*The Harlem and Irish Renaissances*

# The Harlem and Irish Renaissances

*Language, Identity, and Representation*

Tracy Mishkin

Foreword by George Bornstein

University Press of Florida

*Gainesville · Tallahassee · Tampa · Boca Raton · Pensacola · Orlando · Miami · Jacksonville*

Library of Congress Cataloging-in-Publication Data

Mishkin, Tracy.
The Harlem and Irish renaissances: language, identity, and
representation / Tracy Mishkin with a foreword
by George Bornstein.
p. cm.
Includes bibliographical references (p. ) and index.
ISBN 0-8130-1611-8 (hardcover: alk. paper)
1. American literature—Afro-American authors—History and
criticism. 2. English literature—Irish authors—History and
criticism. 3. Literature, Comparative—American and English.
4. Literature, Comparative—English and American. 5. Language
and culture—United States. 6. Afro-Americans—Intellectual life.
7. Language and culture—Ireland. 8. Group identity in literature.
9. Ireland—Intellectual life. 10. Mimesis in literature.
11. Harlem Renaissance. I. Title.
PS153.N5M57    1998
810.9'896073—dc21    98-27017

The University Press of Florida is the scholarly publishing agency
for the State University System of Florida, comprising Florida
A & M University, Florida Atlantic University, Florida Interna-
tional University, Florida State University, University of Central
Florida, University of Florida, University of North Florida,
University of South Florida, and University of West Florida.

University Press of Florida
15 Northwest 15th Street
Gainesville, FL 32611
http://nervm.nerdc.ufl.edu/~upf

*for George Kelley*

# Contents

# Foreword

When in liner notes to a recent CD the contemporary African-American folk-rock singer Laura Love describes her music as "Afro-Celt," or when in an interview the Irish singer Bono cites blues and gospel music among the primary influences on the sound of his rock band U2, they engage in crosscultural constructions that have existed for at least two centuries between those two groups. Explored by Tracy Mishkin in this splendid new study, such connections or "crossings" belong to a new wave of scholarship in the 1990s, which blurs the lines of race and ethnicity that scholarship of the previous two decades tended to keep distinct. The new work takes its cue from theoretical contributions by Homi Bhabha, Cornel West, Werner Sollors, and Henry Louis Gates, among others. It includes recent studies like Susan Gubar's *Racechanges: White Skin, Black Face in American Culture* and Linda Browder's *Ethnic Performance and American Identities*, along with recent collections like Elaine Ginsberg's *Passing and the Fictions of Identity* and Mishkin's own *Literary Influence and African-American Writers*. Far from heralding a return to a less complicated past, the new scholarship instead strives to recomplicate crucial issues in the production of both literature and identity that have a particular pertinence not only to literary study but to some of the most crucial and contested social debates of our day.

Whether welcoming, anxious, or somewhere in between, the new studies suggest in various ways that much art is socially liminal, created often at the intersection of two or more different cultures. Models of purity and separatism of ethnic identity seem less satisfactory than those based on cultural interaction. Yet it would be easy but misleading to compile a list of, say, great African-American writers of the past century who have movingly described such interactions. The list might include, for example, W. E. B. Du Bois in the famous passage of *The Souls of Black Folk* where he invokes sitting with Shakespeare and meeting Balzac, Dumas, Aristotle, and Aurelius; Paul Robeson in his autobiography when he identifies the key influence on his education being his father taking him through Homer and Virgil in the original Greek and Latin; Zora Neale Hurston recounting in *Dust Tracks on a Road* her desire to be an English teacher to impart to others her fervor for English Romantic poets, especially Coleridge; or Ralph Ellison in his great essay "Hidden Name and Complex Fate" identifying his passion for T. S. Eliot's *The Waste Land* as a poem that "seized my mind" and prompted "my conscious education in literature."

But to stop with such attestations might provide too easy a picture of the real stress involved in multicultural creation and response. Perhaps nearer to the mark are two avowals, each well known in its own tradition but whose congruence with the other tradition deserves emphasis here. The first is W. E. B. Du Bois's famous passage on "double consciousness," itself a term continuing the Wordsworthian echo of the opening section of *Souls of Black Folk*:

> One ever feels his twoness,—an American, a Negro; two souls, two thoughts, two unreconciled strivings; two warring ideals in one dark body, whose dogged strength alone keeps it from being torn asunder. The history of the American Negro is the history of this strife. . . . In this merging he wishes neither of the older selves to be lost . . . to be both a Negro and an American . . . to be a co-worker in the kingdom of culture.

Correspondingly, Irish writer W. B. Yeats described his own double consciousness of both Irish and English elements this way in his late essay "A General Introduction for My Work":

> The "Irishry" have preserved their ancient "deposit" through wars which, during the sixteenth and seventeenth centuries, became wars of extermination. No people, Lecky said at the opening of his *Ireland in the Eighteenth Century*, have undergone greater persecution, nor did that persecution altogether cease up to our own day. No people hate as we do in whom that past is always alive, there are moments when hatred poisons my life. . . . Then I remind myself that though mine is the first English marriage I know of in the direct

line, all my family names are English, and that I owe my soul to Shakespeare, to Spenser, and to Blake, perhaps also to William Morris, and to the English language in which I think, speak, and write, that everything I love has come to me through English; my hatred tortures me with love, my love with hate.

Both passages display both the power and the pain of cultural hybridity. Far from unusual, such avowals of multiple allegiance seem the normal condition of writers, and of ourselves. We write as and are members of various groups—whether defined by "race," ethnicity, class, gender, family, religion, or nationality—and yet of a broader community as well. In that sense, Du Bois's noble aspiration is our own: "to be a co-worker in the kingdom of culture."

Coming after a phase of criticism has sought relentlessly to demystify claims of art to "universality," unmasking instead the social contingency of its production and reception, the newer scholarship exemplified in Mishkin's tracing of Irish and African-American connections here suggests that ethnic interaction is the normative state of cultural production, and that fantasies of separatist purity and tradition are themselves urgently in need of demystification. In recent theoretical statements two leading African-American critics have urged just those contentions. Cornell West in his *Prophetic Thought in Modern Times* (1993) writes that "from the very beginning we must call into question any notions of pure traditions or pristine heritages, or any civilization or culture having a monopoly on virtue or insight. Ambiguous legacies, hybrid cultures. By hybrid, of course, we mean cross-cultural fertilization. Every culture that we know is a result of the weaving of antecedent cultures." In a similar vein, Henry Louis Gates, Jr., also uses the metaphor of hybridity in *Loose Canons: Notes on the Culture Wars* (1992): "Pluralism sees culture as porous, dynamic, and interactive, rather than as the fixed property of particular ethnic groups . . . the world we live in is multicultural already. Mixing and hybridity are the rule, not the exception." All culture may be multiculture already, and the task of education may be to reveal the multiculturalism that is already there rather to imagine a separatism that never was on land or sea.

In displaying the multiculturalism of culture, Tracy Mishkin's *The Harlem and Irish Renaissances* provides an outstanding example of what Clifford Geertz calls "thick description." She begins with two chapters historically grounding the two renaissances, with full display of the analogies between them drawn by both participants and outsiders. Mishkin's nuanced portrait acknowledges important differences between Irish and African-American experience up to the early years of our century even while foregrounding the similarities that united them and even caused the Irish Renaissance to be invoked as a model by makers of the Harlem one. Those features included experience of oppression, loss of a traditional language, and lack of control over group representations. In subsequent chapters on language, identity, and the image of the "folk," Mishkin shows how both movements saw links between liberation, linguistic construction, and regaining of control over the means and content of representation. At once a sensitive recuperation of a past cultural moment and a contribution to our current one, Mishkin's study both participates in our present national conversation and prepares the way for future ones.

GEORGE BORNSTEIN

# Preface

Renaissance is a beautiful word. We use it even when
we are not sure what has been reborn.

*Mary Lou Kohfeldt*

While I was a graduate student at the University of Michigan, I heard that a black theater troupe in North Carolina had been influenced by Ireland's Abbey Theatre during the Harlem Renaissance. Intrigued, I began to look for evidence. Although I did not find any,[1] I did find other instances of influence involving the Harlem and Irish renaissances as well as a great many similarities between them. However, despite the numerous comparisons of these two movements made in newspaper articles earlier in this century, little scholarly research has been done on the subject. The connection is occasionally established in works about African-American theater or the Harlem Renaissance, most notably in Nathan Huggins's 1971 work, *Harlem Renaissance,* in which he referred twice to the difficulties faced by both Irish and African-American writers (203, 231).[2] Furthermore, in 1981 *Éire-Ireland* published a brief article by Brian Gallagher comparing the Harlem and Irish renaissances, and in 1990 C. L. Innes published a monograph comparing African and Irish literature that contains several references to an African-American and Irish connection. Generally speaking, however, the similarities have been little remarked since the Harlem movement ended. The aim of this work is to revisit a paradigm that seems at one time to have been well known in intellectual circles, both black and white, and suggest how it might continue to be useful today.

Because the Harlem and Irish renaissances were, in Cary Wintz's phrase, "state[s] of mind" (2) as much as movements for literary and social change, many works on the renaissances begin by attempting to establish parameters: when these movements began and ended, how they should be studied, what type of texts and which writers should be included. Scholars must define Irish literature—does it include literature in Irish and English?—and decide whether the Harlem movement represents African-American literature or literature by African-American people.

I have left extended consideration of these issues to those whose work focuses on one movement or the other, but one issue that it seems useful to address at the outset is the question of dating. It is generally agreed that the Irish Renaissance began in the mid-1880s, as a group of young, mostly Anglo-Irish cultural nationalists gathered around the aging revolutionary John O'Leary, and that it ended around the time of the establishment of the puritanical Irish Free State in 1922. The beginning of the Harlem Renaissance is usually set in the early 1920s, when African-American writers began to congregate in New York City, and most scholars agree that the Great Depression of the 1930s slowly ended it. For the purposes of this work, I have occasionally considered writers, such as James Joyce, who wrote during one of these renaissances but did not affiliate themselves with them and writers, such as Paul Laurence Dunbar, who flourished shortly before these movements and served as important precursors. My approach involves a thematic comparison rather than an exhaustive survey; therefore, certain writers will receive a different amount of attention than they might in a more traditional study of one movement or the other. I have attempted to keep the chronology clear as I move back and forth in time between these two literary renaissances. However, despite the fact that the Irish Renaissance largely predates the cultural upheaval and accomplishments of the early years of the twentieth century and the Harlem Renaissance generally postdates them, the participants in the renaissances focussed on the similarities, not the differences, to an extent that often feels quite ahistorical. Yet this should not be surprising, for—Virginia Woolf's comment on human character changing in December 1910 notwithstanding—prejudice and discrimination continued along remarkably similar lines an ocean and a generation away.[3]

A few words about terminology. When a quotation includes an outdated racial term such as "negro" or "Aframerican," I have retained the original usage. For my own purposes, I use "African-American" and "black" interchangeably. By "Anglo-Irish" I mean Irish Protestants of

English or Scottish descent, and by "Ascendancy" I mean the Anglo-Irish power elite after the late eighteenth century. I refer to the English and Irish languages, as well as to African-American and Hiberno-English dialects of English.

I would like to thank those who made the publication of this work possible, primarily the members of my dissertation committee—George Bornstein and Rafia Zafar, my co-chairs, and Leo McNamara and Janet Hart, my third and outside readers. I have also received helpful suggestions from Richard Bizot, Zack Bowen, Tony Hale, and Joseph Skerrett and a great deal of support from my colleagues at Georgia College and State University.

Finally, I have been extremely fortunate to have George Kelley in my life, both to offer insightful comments on my research and to take the edge off my workaholic tendencies.

Grateful acknowledgment is made to the following for permission to reprint previously published material.

Alfred A. Knopf: Four lines from "Red Silk Stockings," from *Collected Poems*, by Langston Hughes. Copyright 1994 by the Estate of Langston Hughes. Reprinted by permission of Alfred A. Knopf, Inc.

Scribner: Eight lines from "September, 1913," reprinted with the permission of Scribner, a Division of Simon & Schuster, from *The Collected Works of W. B. Yeats*, volume 1, *The Poems*, revised and edited by Richard J. Finneran (New York: Scribner, 1997).

William L. Clements Library: Photograph of *Harper's Weekly* cover illustration, December 9, 1876. By permission of William L. Clements Library, Ann Arbor, Michigan.

*Introduction*

# "How Black Sees Green and Red"
## Renaissance Eclecticism

Tim Murphy's gon' walkin' wid Maggie O'Neill, / O chone!
*Paul Laurence Dunbar, African-American poet*

O! George, you may, without a blush, confess your
love for the Octoroon.
*Dion Boucicault, Irish playwright*

The Abbey Theatre's 1911 tour of the United States caused unrest in several cities over John Synge's *Playboy of the Western World:* many Irish Americans felt that the play inaccurately represented rural Irish people, especially women. Their counterparts in Ireland had already condemned Synge's work along with other works of the Irish Renaissance: in 1907 the *Freeman's Journal* described *The Playboy* as "unmitigated, protracted libel on Irish peasant men and, worse still upon Irish peasant girlhood" (qtd. in Greene and Stephens 257). However, even as eggs and potatoes were hurled at the actors (Dalsimer 77), the Abbey's representations of Irish life caught the imagination of those Americans interested in exploring the various facets of their own national identity, including several people, black and white, who went on to participate in the Harlem Renaissance of the 1920s. They noted the many similarities between Irish culture and history and those of African Americans, and they advocated following the Irish model for literary renaissance and social change.

In 1911, borrowing ideas from and comparing one's movement to other ethnic groups struggling for political freedom and cultural identity had been common in Europe and in the Americas for more than a hundred years, indeed since the rise of nationalism in the late eighteenth century. As Benedict Anderson writes in *Imagined Communities*, "when history made it possible, in 1811, for Venezuelan revolutionaries to draw up a constitution for the First Venezuelan Republic, they saw nothing slavish in borrowing verbatim from the Constitution of the United States of America. For what the men in Philadelphia had written was in the Venezuelans' eyes not something North American, but rather something of universal truth and value" (192). Thus, the influence of the Irish Renaissance on African-American writers and intellectuals was not unusual, despite the fact that black people and Irish Americans were not on the best of terms in America's cities. As Thomas Sowell relates, "perhaps the worst relations between any two groups in American history have been between the Irish and the Negroes" (38). Because African Americans and Irish Americans often coexisted at the bottom of the socioeconomic ladder in the late nineteenth and early twentieth centuries, they tended to clash as they tried to move up. Lerone Bennett states that "[t]he struggle between the Irish immigrants and black workers was particularly acrimonious. At that point [the mid-nineteenth century] and for several decades thereafter, the Irish were considered 'white niggers' and were subjected to the same indignities as blacks" (179).[1] Despite the generally poor relations between their communities, a number of black and Irish intellectuals found common ground.

Because of the popularity of the Abbey Theatre tours and the similarities between African-American and Irish experiences, the Irish Renaissance became an important influence on black writers; however, many other comparisons were available to and eagerly used by both peoples, and, not surprisingly, some degree of overlap occurred. Both movements found similarities between themselves and Russian, Hungarian, Scottish, and Italian political and/or literary revivals, but one of the most popular and detailed common comparisons was to Jewish people. Like others before them—for example, the Puritans—members of both renaissances compared their movements to various aspects of Jewish politics, culture, and history. A detailed examination of these relationships will shed light on the phenomenon of nationalist eclecticism.

**The Jews: A Model for Black-Irish Comparisons**

During slavery, many African Americans identified with the biblical Jews, specifically with the Hebrew slaves who won their freedom and built a nation after much suffering in the land of Egypt. The culture of black resistance was constructed largely around the people and places of the Hebrew Bible: the songs urged "Go down, Moses" and spoke of "Crossing over Jordan." However, like many Christians then and today, the slaves saw the Hebrews not so much as Jews than as proto-Christians. This helps explain why, despite the black slave/Hebrew slave identification, a number of spirituals also blamed the Jews for the death of Jesus (Lester 68–69).

This partial identification was generally unidirectional. Like most white Americans, American Jews tended to be antislavery if they lived in the North and proslavery if they lived in the South. Even northern Jews were not usually involved in the abolitionist movement because history had taught the Jewish people that "[r]apid political change often meant new perils. Mass, uncontrolled political movements could always turn into an attack against the Jews" (Kaufman 20). However, with the advent of the second wave of Jewish immigration in the 1880s, this largely changed. The new immigrants were more open to advocating social change because of their own experiences with reform and their exposure to socialism in Eastern Europe, not to mention the increasing anti-Semitism of the United States (Kaufman 23).

Jewish philanthropists and African-American intellectuals built strong ties in the early twentieth century. Many of the white members of the NAACP and the Urban League were Jewish, including Amy and Joel Spingarn and Julius Rosenwald. To Jewish people confronting institutional anti-Semitism, helping the fledgling civil rights movement seemed both a means of and a corollary to carrying out their own agenda. As David Lewis puts it, "Being of use to the Negro was becoming virtually a specialty of the second most abused Americans of the early twentieth century" (102–3, 100). Although they were likely to be more sympathetic than other white Americans, Jewish people were not exempt from racist attitudes and practices. Blumstein's, the largest department store in Harlem, originally refused to hire African Americans even as elevator operators and later balked at hiring black sales and clerical staff, claiming that the owner's support of African-American charities and hiring of black menial labor were sufficient.

Despite these problems, many black Americans made the transition from identifying with biblical Jews to admiring contemporary ones. Beginning with Frederick Douglass, African-American intellectuals lobbied for black emulation of Jewish practices and for stronger ties between the black and Jewish communities (Lester 70–72). In the 1910s, James Weldon Johnson used his editorial position at the *New York Age* to propound his belief that African Americans should emulate Jewish political, financial, and organizational achievements. "There is a parallel between the condition of the Jewish race and of the Negro race," he wrote, "which is often remarkably striking" ("Difference"). Similar to the common Jewish belief, Johnson saw the Jewish civil rights struggle as potentially beneficial to African Americans, writing that "[t]he wise thing for the Negro to do is to form as close an alliance with the Jew as is possible, so that the latter in fighting for his own rights will, in some degree, fight for ours also" ("National Guard"). Johnson perceived the Jewish presence in American politics and business to be so strong that anti-Semitic Americans kept their sentiments to themselves and did not openly discriminate against Jewish people. He believed that in the few instances in which discrimination occurred, it was immediately and successfully challenged by a powerful Jewish lobby. He hoped that African Americans could emulate Jewish people and reach "the place in this country where people dare not discriminate against them no matter what feelings of prejudice they may have" ("Prejudice"). Jewish people did have more success than did African Americans at ending discriminatory practices in the early twentieth century, but they by no means enjoyed the overwhelming rate of success Johnson envisioned. His misperception of the strength of American Jews seems the result of wishful thinking about the future of his own race as well as of stereotypes about Jewish financial and political power.

While Johnson's articles evince positive if overly optimistic ideas about blacks and Jews, the Jamaican-born writer Claude McKay's 1938 article in the *Amsterdam News* suggests the ambivalence prevalent in the relations between the African-American and Jewish communities. Responding to an editorial in the Zionist journal *Jewish Frontier* that called for African Americans and Jewish people to "purge their ranks of all prejudice and intolerance" and unite, McKay wrote that Jewish people needed to stop their discrimination against African Americans first. He felt that Jewish racism was a much larger problem than black anti-Semitism; in fact, McKay called "anti-Semitism" a misnomer for the "friction" his people had with individual Jews. He believed that the term "anti-Semitism" was most properly applied to "an organized political and social movement of gentiles against Jews . . . identifiable with extreme nationalism or extreme fanaticism" such as that found in Nazi Germany ("M'Kay Tells of Jews" 17). McKay wanted an alliance between the African-American and Jewish communities, but he was not willing to admit the existence of black anti-Semitism. Like many African Americans, Johnson and McKay accepted spurious notions about Jewish power and Black-Jewish relations that, along with Jewish racism, hampered the formation of even stronger ties between the two communities.

A somewhat similar situation existed in Ireland, where many nationalists drew parallels between Jewish and Irish history, but anti-Semitism plagued those Jews (3,769 in 1901, according to Hyman) who walked the streets of Ireland rather than the pages of the Bible (160). Irish nationalists pointed to their common desire for a homeland, their ancient languages, their proud pasts, their prophets Charles Stewart Parnell and Moses, and their similar claims to the protection of God during oppressive times (Kenner, *Colder Eye* 194). Meanwhile, events like the 1904 Limerick boycott of Jewish merchants, which lasted for a year and drove out two-thirds of the city's Jewish population, served as a reminder that whatever salient parallels "the chosen people" offered "the island of saints and scholars," anti-Semitism was practiced by many Irish people (Ellmann 373).[2]

Despite the ambivalences Ireland offered its Jewish inhabitants, life there was better than in the shtetl and the ghetto. Jewish people sometimes received special considerations; for example, women in need of the mikvah, a ritual immersion, were the only Dubliners allowed to use the Tara Street Baths during a water shortage in 1914 (J. O'Brien 102). Most anti-Semitic acts were petty and not physically violent, unlike those in Eastern Europe, from which much of Ireland's Jewish population had recently emigrated. When Irish leaders such as Arthur Griffith and Father Creagh of Limerick waxed anti-Semitic, other prominent Irish people like Michael Davitt denounced them, stating their pride in Ireland's reputation for harmonious relations with Jewish people and pointing out the hypocrisy of one oppressed group attacking another (Hyman 213). As in the relationship between African Americans and Jewish people, some of the more sympathetic Irish people were writers and intellectuals. While living in Paris, James Joyce used his connections to help sixteen Jewish refugees to safety after the Austrian Anschluss of 1938 (Ellmann 709).

An important difference between African-American and Irish attitudes toward Jewish people grew from the fact that, because of their small numbers and relative obscurity, Irish Jews were in no way as politically useful to other Irish people as American Jews were to black people. Very few of the Jews in Ireland became involved in politics, partly because many Irish Catholics did not consider them Irish (Hyman 176) and partly because history had taught them, as it had taught their American counterparts, that large grassroots political movements could easily become pogroms. With the notable exception of Jacob Elyan, advisor to various factions in the nationalist movement, most Irish Jews concerned themselves with their families and their religious community, not their nation. Thus, no reasons existed for either an alliance or the tensions that accompanied similar alliances in the United States (Hyman 200–2). In general, by the times of the renaissances, Irish people seem more likely to have referred to a Jewish educational or religious tradition and African-American commentators more likely to have noted contemporary political similarities, because different aspects of Jewish life were more manifest in the one milieu than in the another.

Regardless of the ambivalence in African-American and Irish attitudes toward Jewish people, intellectuals in both renaissances drew parallels to their own causes in Jewish history and culture. In *The New Negro*, Alain Locke compared growing pan-African sentiments in the African diaspora to the Zionist movement: "Harlem," he said, "is the home of the Negro's 'Zionism,'" suggesting that it was a center for the diverse elements of African-descended people's lives and a place of potential unity (14). Just as Jews from many countries were united by their longing for a homeland and a refuge from persecution, many people of African descent came together in Harlem and discussed their relation to their ancestral home. Locke phrased it thus: "As with the Jew, persecution is making the Negro international" (14).

Douglas Hyde used a similar technique in "The Necessity for De-Anglicising Ireland" to draw the attention of lecture-goers to the sorry state of the Irish language. He outlined several reforms necessary to "bring about a tone of thought which would make it disgraceful for an educated Irishman . . . to be ignorant of his own language—would make it at least as disgraceful as for an educated Jew to be quite ignorant of Hebrew" (*Language* 161). Hyde wished to change Irish attitudes about the Irish language from scorn to reverence, a feeling similar to that found in Judaism for Hebrew.

Leslie Catherine Sanders suggests that an interesting nexus of African-American, Jewish, and Irish ways came in the theater, as black dramatists perceived Irish and Jewish models for their own movement. The Irish model addressed a mainstream audience, while the Jewish theater in New York "remained insistently discrete" from mainstream America in the early twentieth century, producing plays, often in Yiddish, on themes largely of interest to Jewish people (10). Both approaches appealed to African Americans: the former because it allowed playwrights to correct misrepresentations of their people found on the American stage, and the latter because it allowed them to address more clearly and deeply the concerns of African-American audiences. Alain Locke and Montgomery Gregory's 1927 anthology, *Plays of Negro Life,* followed the Irish mainstreaming model: at least eight of the twenty plays were written by white dramatists, and Gregory's introduction situated black drama within American theater. On the other hand, Willis Richardson's two anthologies published in the 1930s, *Plays and Pageants from the Life of the Negro* and *Negro History in Thirteen Plays,* were directed toward African-American communities. His anthologies consisted largely of historical pageants and plays, and Carter G. Woodson's introduction to the second one argued for more black-authored plays, stating that white dramatists could not "think black" (qtd. in Sanders 11). Whether or not whites could "think black," African Americans and Irish people showed that they could think Jewish, drawing inspiration from Jewish people for a variety of political and cultural projects.

Going beyond seeing parallels or gaining inspiration, during both the Harlem and the Irish renaissances writers sometimes used Jewish characters to address issues that concerned them and their communities. For example, James Joyce believed that Jewish and Irish people had a number of characteristics in common, including impulsiveness, a tendency toward fantasy, and associative rather than rational thought (Ellmann 395). In addition to these rather standard primitivist notions (which he also applied to women), Joyce considered certain more realistic aspects of early-twentieth-century Jewish life to be similar to his own: the isolation from society that creates close family ties and the interest in textuality and writing (Nadel 16, 5). He created Leopold Bloom, a deracinated Jewish Dubliner, to explore some of his personal and political concerns in *Ulysses.* Like the self-exiled Joyce, Bloom cannot go home in any sense of the word: his house is occupied by his adulterous wife Molly, he is scorned as a Jew although he has been baptized, and there is no Jewish homeland in 1904. Bloom says of Zionism, "Nothing doing. Still an idea behind it" (60). Perhaps Joyce would say the same of Irish nationalism.

Although Irish Jews rarely participated in politics, Joyce inserted Bloom into the nationalist milieu: "as a matter of strict history," he makes him return Parnell's hat after it is knocked off in a crowd, and he also creates one of the few anachronisms in the novel by having Bloom coin the term "Sinn Fein" for Arthur Griffith, who did not actually use the term publicly until later that year (664, 335; Thornton 138). Joyce's use of anachronism and his claim that fiction is "strict history" in order to create a space for Bloom in Irish politics parallels his satirical litany of Irish-Jewish similarities in the "Ithaca" chapter, which reads in part as follows: "their archeological, genealogical, hagiographical, exegetical, homilectic, toponomastic, historical and religious literatures comprising the work of rabbis and culdees, Torah, Talmud . . . Book of the Dun Cow . . . Book of Kells" (688). Although Joyce believed that certain parallels existed, he felt that some nationalists took them to a foolish extreme. *Ulysses* both suggests the similarities and rejects their overuse. Unlike the image of Jews held by many Irish people, Bloom is a modern, not a biblical, character, and his Jewish identity is often tenuous.

Just as Joyce used a Jewish character to explore his personal concerns and criticize the excesses of his people, in her 1939 work *Moses, Man of the Mountain*, Zora Neale Hurston borrowed Moses from the Jewish tradition in order to study the problems facing African Americans. Hurston stated in her introduction that, in addition to his image as a Hebrew lawgiver, "Africa has her mouth on Moses . . . all across Africa, America, the West Indies, there are tales of the powers of Moses and great worship of him and his powers."[3] Hurston wanted to give a post-bellum spin to the story of the liberation of the Israelites from bondage in Egypt which had played such a powerful role in antebellum African-American life. To depict an African-American Moses, Hurston altered the diction of the biblical narrative; for example, Miriam sends her baby brother onto the Nile with the following prayer: "Nile, youse such a great big river and he is such a little bitty thing. Show him some mercy, please" (39). Her Africanization of the Hebrews allowed Hurston to suggest parallels between the condition of the newly freed Israelites and that of post-emancipation black people. In addition, it allowed her to raise questions of import to African Americans: What are the burdens of freedom? Can one be truly free while following a charismatic leader? What are the implications of an emphasis on racial purity? (McDowell x-xi, xiii-xvi).

While Hurston used a biblical figure to comment on modern times, Alice Dunbar-Nelson, the widow of Paul Laurence Dunbar, created a contemporary Jewish character in her play *Mine Eyes Have Seen*. Chris, a young African-American whose father was shot defending his home from arsonists, is drafted to serve in World War I. Reluctant to fight for a country that has denied his family equal protection under the law and equal participation in society, he must be convinced by his siblings and friends, one of whom is a young Jewish man named Jake. Jake claims that although the Jews have been persecuted in many lands, "we're loyal always to the country where we live and serve" (274). He urges Chris to consider the future, to set aside present and past injustices in the hope of a better tomorrow. At the end of the play, Chris seems to have come around to this point of view, which was shared by many—though not all—prominent African Americans.

Joyce's Bloom, Hurston's Moses, and Dunbar-Nelson's Jake, Jewish figures created by Irish and African-American artists, symbolize the ability of Harlem and Irish renaissance artists and intellectuals to fruitfully compare themselves to other peoples who faced discrimination. Although these comparisons were sometimes rooted in stereotypes and other types of misinformation and African Americans and Irish people did not always coexist peacefully with their Jewish neighbors, the inspiration these comparisons gave to the renaissance writers suggests their continuing usefulness.

## Early Black-Irish Comparisons

In addition to comparing themselves to the Jews, African Americans and Irish people drew parallels between and gained literary and political inspiration from their common experiences, stereotypes and street brawls notwithstanding. In Ireland, these comparisons date back to at least the late eighteenth century. The *Northern Star*, the newspaper of the United Irishmen in Belfast, frequently referred to the condition of Ireland as "slavery" and published poems such as "The Negroe's Complaint," which appeared in 1792:

> Slaves of gold, whose sordid dealings
> >　　　 Tarnish all your boasted pow'rs,
> Prove that you have human feelings,
> >　　　 Ere you proudly question ours! (qtd. in Thuente 91)

The poem suggests that white people, who often claimed that blacks were subhuman, as the English often did the Irish, ought to be careful that their actions do not reflect their own shortcomings.

In the early to mid-nineteenth century, Daniel O'Connell continued the black-Irish comparison when he suggested similarities between the struggle for Catholic emancipation and repeal of the Act of Union between England and Ireland and the abolitionists' fight against the slave trade. O'Connell spoke out so strongly against slavery that he drew criticism in Ireland and America for not making the repeal movement his paramount concern, and he lost much of his American support when he would not compromise his humanitarian principles. In a March 1845 speech to the Repeal Association, O'Connell thundered, "I want no American aid if it comes across the Atlantic stained in Negro blood" (O'Ferrall 44–45). O'Connell once introduced Frederick Douglass at a Repeal meeting as "the Black O'Connell of the United States" (Allen 178). However, not all Irish politicians were comfortable with even occasional comparisons between their people and African-descended slaves: Arthur Griffith spent more than a quarter of his 1913 preface to John Mitchel's 1854 *Jail Journal* defending Mitchel's proslavery views and indignantly added, "as if excuse were needed for an Irish Nationalist declining to hold the negro his peer in right" (xiv). Mitchel belonged to the Young Ireland movement, which argued that American support of Irish freedom would be compromised by an abolitionist stance. Although Irish people did not always agree about the similarity of their situation to that of American slaves or find it politic to compare them publicly, the subject was hotly debated for decades.

Early comparisons of a sort also occurred in Irish literature. Four days after the hanging of John Brown in 1859, a play by the prolific and popular Irish playwright Dion Boucicault entitled *The Octoroon; Or, Life in Louisiana* opened in New York. *The Octoroon* was a melodrama that aimed to please pro- and antislavery factions: the author presented both bucolic plantation scenes and the horrors of slavery. Although Boucicault straddled the fence on the slavery question, the play differed enough from standard nineteenth-century depictions of African Americans for Montgomery Gregory to praise it in *Plays of Negro Life*. Gregory wrote that *The Octoroon* represented a welcome respite from the flood of minstrel shows popular in the second half of the nineteenth century, as it "accustomed the theatre-going public to the experience of seeing a number of Negro characters in other than the conventional 'darkey' rôles" (409–10). Gregory exaggerated: the title character, Zoe, is the only non-"darkey" character, although one was enough to infuriate a New York theater critic who pronounced the play abolitionist propaganda and Zoe an impossible creation ("'The Octoroon'" 1).[4]

Since Gregory's comments in 1927, other critics have also distorted Boucicault's attitudes and accomplishments, overstating the degree to which he perceived a connection between Irish and African-American oppressions. For example, biographer Richard Fawkes stated that "[a]s an Irishman, a member of a subjugated nation, Boucicault felt keenly the indignity of slavery, of one race being beholden to another" (109). Fawkes does not successfully substantiate this claim with Boucicault's writings. In fact, in an 1861 letter to the *London Times,* Boucicault claimed that his years of residence in Louisiana had shown him that slavery was not as terrible as the abolitionists asserted: "I found the slaves, as a race, a happy, gentle, kindly-treated population, and the restraints upon their liberty so slight as to be rarely perceptible" (5). Fawkes only quotes part of this letter, making Boucicault appear more opposed to slavery than he was. It may not be a coincidence that Boucicault's plays written in the decade or so after the production of *The Octoroon* included his most famous Irish comic political melodramas, *The Colleen Bawn, Arrah-na-Pogue,* and *The Shaughraun;* however, the assertion that Boucicault explicitly connected African-American and Irish oppressions remains conjectural.

When black Americans began to speak out for their people's freedom in the mid-nineteenth century, for many the Irish connection came readily to mind. During his 1845 lecture tour of Ireland, Frederick Douglass drew strong parallels between the struggles of the two peoples. In a letter published in the American abolitionist newspaper *The Liberator,* Douglass wrote, "I see much here to remind me of my former condition, and I confess I should be ashamed to lift my voice against American slavery, but that I know the cause of humanity is one the world over. He who really and truly feels for the American slave cannot steel his heart to the woes of others" (qtd. in Bornstein 174). The early black nationalist Martin R. Delany wrote in 1852 that black Americans had in common with the Irish, among others, their status as "a nation within a nation" (12). As with Irish people, however, African Americans did not always see these comparisons similarly. Like Douglass, Harriet Jacobs drew a comparison between black slaves and Irish paupers, but her conclusion was different. In a letter written about 1852 to the abolitionist Amy Post she said that it is "far better to have been one of the starving poor of Ireland . . . than to have been a slave with the curse of slavery stamped upon yourself and Children" (232).

Cultural outsiders also compared the two peoples, but they often posited inferiority as the terms of comparison. For example, the late-nineteenth-century English ethnologist John Beddoe claimed that his Index of Nigrescence showed that as one moved from east to west in the British Isles, the people became more and more Negroid, sporting dark complexions, large jaws, and long nostrils. Although his Index was scientifically specious, Beddoe's mass of data, the result of more than thirty years of fieldwork, was highly convincing to his audience (L. Curtis 19–20). On the other hand, Gustave de Beaumont, a French traveler, wrote in 1839: "I have seen the Indian in his forests, and the negro in his chains, and thought, as I contemplated their pitiable condition, that I saw the very extreme of human wretchedness; but I did not then know the condition of unfortunate Ireland" (268).[5]

Many white American comparisons followed Beddoe rather than de Beaumont. In 1876, for example, *Harper's Weekly* published a cover illustration by Thomas Nast entitled "The Ignorant Vote: Honors Are Easy," which depicts an African-American man and an Irish-American man sitting on a balanced scale. The cartoon asserts that African Americans as new Republicans and Irish Americans as new Democrats will have an equally deleterious effect on the country's electoral process. Both of these people are drawn with facial features more reminiscent of apes than of human beings, a common device for nineteenth-century illustrators wishing to represent Irish (or Irish-American) and black people as subhuman.[6]

### Americans Make Use of Ireland

In the early twentieth century, American representations began to change as black people began writing in increasing numbers and as news of the Irish Renaissance spread. In addition to derogatory or pitying comparisons, artistic and political ones emerged, with both white and black Americans noting the potential usefulness of the Irish Renaissance for those interested in portraying African-American lives.

Although their depictions of Irish life had come under fire at home as well as abroad, the Abbey's use of folk culture and of Irish dialects was intended to create more accurate portrayals of Irish people than those found on the British stage. As the theater's co-founders W. B. Yeats and

Cover of *Harper's Weekly,* December 9, 1876. By permission of the William Clements Library, Ann Arbor, Michigan.

Augusta Gregory wrote in an 1898 manifesto, "We will show that Ireland is not the home of buffoonery and of easy sentiment, as it has been represented" (Gregory, *Theatre* 9). The Irish Renaissance inspired Americans to attempt a similar type of literature using black culture as a base. In 1926, W. E. B. Du Bois marked the founding of the Krigwa Players Little Negro Theatre by publishing an essay that put forth a definition of a black theater movement. It stated, in part, that "[t]he plays of a real Negro theatre must be [about us]. That is, they must have plots which reveal Negro life as it is" ("Krigwa" 134). Du Bois did not mention the Abbey Theatre in his article, but the Krigwa Players were part of the Little Theatre movement that was engendered by the Abbey's American tours.

Unfortunately for both the Harlem and Irish renaissances, many community leaders were interested not in realistic representations but in idealized portraits because they wanted to enlist literature to fight prejudice. This clashed with the writers' desire for artistic freedom, which did not necessarily favor realism either. For these reasons, the dreams of Yeats, Gregory, and Du Bois were not easily fulfilled. The Harlem Renaissance's depictions of the folk proved to be as controversial as those of the Irish movement.

Ridgely Torrence, a versatile white author not well known today, provides an early example of a writer being inspired by the Irish Renaissance to produce literature on African-American subjects. Torrence had seen the Abbey Theatre's 1911 productions in New York City, and, as he explained in 1917, "The parallel . . . with the Irish race and its national drama, made a deep impression on me. I wanted to make the experiment, and try to contribute something, if I could, to a possible Negro drama, as vital and as charming as the Irish" ("The New Negro Theatre" 80). His play *Granny Maumee* was written and first produced in 1914, and, in 1917, two of Torrence's other "Negro plays," *The Rider of Dreams* and *Simon the Cyrenian,* joined it on the New York stage at the Garden Theatre. The latter production was notable for its use of African-American actors, at that time still a rarity outside of amateur black theater. Despite his reference to Irish drama as "charming," Torrence's plays were often quite serious. In *Granny Maumee,* for example, he explored the issue of racial purity from a black perspective, an unusual approach for a white author and one that made his audiences uncomfortable (Gale 140).

Torrence's works were well received by both white and black audiences. Several white critics called them significant and compared them to the plays of the Irish Renaissance. After the 1914 production, Carl Van Vechten, future Harlem Renaissance promoter, wrote that he hoped *Granny Maumee* would not be "a flash in the pan," calling it "as important an event in our [American] theater as the production of the first play of Synge was to the Irish movement" ("Beginnings of a Negro Drama" 1114). In 1917 Zona Gale, a novelist and journalist, stated in a review in *Theatre Arts Magazine* of Torrence's plays that "[t]o do for the negro theatrically what has been done for the Irish by the Irish Theatre movement is magnificently worthwhile. This is to interpret to the public—and perhaps to itself—a race never yet understood, in a land which is not of its own choosing" (139). Journalist Heywood Broun echoed Gale's comments in a *New York Tribune* article, stating that until the production of Torrence's work, "negro life ha[d] meant little to the stage but burnt cork, lumbago, and the word 'massa'" (11).

White reviewers like Van Vechten, Gale, and Broun hoped that Torrence's plays would usher in a new and important form of American drama and improve the extant dramatic representations of African Americans, and they often drew explicit connections to the Irish theater movement to make their points. African Americans also reviewed Torrence's plays, but the Irish theater connection received less attention than Torrence's respectful presentation of black lives. For example, James Weldon Johnson wrote in the *New York Age,* an African-American newspaper, that "[i]t is almost amazing to think how Mr. Torrence . . . could write plays of Negro life with such intimate knowledge, with such deep insight and sympathy" ("The Negro and the Drama"). On the other hand, Lester Walton, the *Age*'s drama critic, concluded a largely favorable review by taking Torrence to task for using dialect for all of his characters, because he felt that it was "hardly probable that *Dr. Williams,* with a college education, would employ Negro dialect in conversation" ("Negro Actors").

Reviewers of the 1910s, black and white alike, generally found Torrence's work realistic and sincere. Few expressed a concern that he might have experienced difficulty depicting African-American lives. One anonymous essayist did say that because he or she had only seen reviews by white people, "it was too early to conclude whether, like Synge, Torrence [had] penetrated the real psychology of a race" ("Beginnings of

a Negro Drama" 1114). As time passed, more African Americans preferred black depictions of black characters—Du Bois's 1926 article says a
Negro theater must have Negro authors—but in 1917, serious dramatic
representation of African Americans was so new that merely using a
black cast met most critics' desires for realistic representation.[7]

Although by the 1920s black representations of black lives were more
in demand, African-American intellectuals were comfortable with borrowing ideas from other cultures. In the decade after Torrence's second
production of "Negro plays," they not only took up the comparison to
the Irish dramatic movement but also expanded it to include other genres
and extra-literary phenomena. In 1925, Alain Locke wrote in the introduction to the *New Negro* anthology that "[w]ithout pretense to [its]
political significance, Harlem has the same rôle to play for the New
Negro as Dublin has had for the New Ireland" (7). Locke suggested a
largely cultural connection, but both political and cultural comparisons
were made by other African-American writers, intellectuals, and politicians.

Dramatist Willis Richardson initiated the literary comparisons in his
1919 article "The Hope of a Negro Drama." After explaining his definition of "Negro plays," that is, those that surpass mere "plays with Negro
characters" and propaganda plays and, instead, show "the soul of the
people," he called the Irish theater movement "an excellent model, and
one by which we ought to profit" (338). Richardson exhorted African
Americans to build a "Negro Drama," stating that Ireland had built a
respected national drama with a much smaller population as a resource.
He looked forward to the day when "a company of Negro Players with
Negro Plays" would tour America and Europe, much as the Abbey
Theatre had toured Ireland and the United States (339). However,
Richardson does not discuss the controversies over the Abbey Theatre's
representations of Irish people. He was either not aware of them, which
seems unlikely, given the reception of the Abbey tours, or the company's
accomplishments were more important to him than the fact that "the
soul of the people" was highly contested.

In the early 1920s, James Weldon Johnson began to apply Irish ideas
to black poetry. In the preface to his 1922 anthology, *The Book of
American Negro Poetry,* he wrote of his desire for African-American
poets to set aside dialect poetry in favor of less restrictive forms:

> What the colored poet in the United States needs to do is something
> like what Synge did for the Irish; he needs to find a form that will

express the racial spirit by symbols from within rather than by symbols from without, such as the mere mutilation of English spelling and pronunciation. He needs a form that is freer and larger than dialect, but which will still hold the racial flavor; a form expressing the imagery, the idioms, the peculiar turns of thought, and the distinctive humor and pathos, too, of the Negro, but which will also be capable of voicing the deepest and highest emotions and aspirations, and allow of the widest range of subjects and the widest scope of treatment. (xl-xli)

Johnson found dialect poetry a limited form, allowing only the expression of "humor and pathos." He was not opposed to the use of African-American dialects per se, but to the "limitations on Negro dialect [poetry] imposed by the fixing effects of long convention," that is, the association with "'possums . . . [and] watermelons" (xxxix–xl). Johnson felt that the problems with dialect could be resolved by an approach similar to Synge's that would accent standard English with the idioms of African-American speech. In 1927 he published *God's Trombones*, a collection of African-American sermons rendered as poetry, in which he attempted to follow his own advice to black writers. In the introduction to this volume, Johnson went so far as to reprint his comments about Synge from his earlier book, declaring, "because I cannot say it better, I quote" (8). Like Richardson, Johnson focussed on accomplishments rather than controversies. Synge was, however, often at the center of the storms surrounding the Abbey, as his dialect and characters were literary inventions in a country hungry for and expecting realistic representations of speech and person, and his irreverence and biting social commentary ruffled not a few feathers. His work remains controversial today.

Alain Locke was among the most frequent commentators on the Harlem and Irish Renaissances, discussing such similarities between the two movements as their urban bases, their use of folk cultures, and the responses of their audiences. Although in the introduction to *The New Negro* Locke discounted any political comparison between the two movements, his dismissal of politics did not extend to a dismissal of controversy. In fact, he seems more aware than Johnson or Richardson of the problems the Irish Renaissance had faced. Later in the same work, in an essay entitled "Negro Youth Speaks," he explained why the fledgling Harlem Renaissance was garnering mixed reviews in African-American communities: "Just as with the Irish Renaissance, there were the riots and controversies over Synge's folk plays and other frank realisms of the younger school, so we are having and will have turbulent discussions and dissatisfaction with the stories, plays and poems of the younger Negro group" (50). Locke noted that, just as in Ireland, those who wanted literature primarily to fight prejudice were uncomfortable with the "frank realisms" of writers such as Jean Toomer, Zora Neale Hurston, Willis Richardson, and Langston Hughes because they feared their work would cast all African Americans in a negative light. Writers in both movements wanted the freedom to choose their own subject matter, but whether that meant Synge's peasants or Hurston's, many Irish people and African Americans were angered by them.

The Irish Renaissance served as both exhortation and explanation for African-American writers and intellectuals: the Abbey Theatre's work suggested the use of folk plays and mediated dialect to Richardson and Johnson, and the Irish movement's negative experiences helped Locke explain similar occurrences to African Americans. However, the examples given here seem to suggest that their knowledge of Irish literature was limited to drama, and their knowledge of drama to John Synge's work. Synge was certainly well known, but other less famous Irish writers inspired black authors as well: Countee Cullen, for example, felt poetically revitalized after attending a Parisian party at which he met several Irish poets (Ferguson 119–20). In a poem entitled "After a Visit," he wrote:

> I had walked two seasons through, and moved among
> Strange ways and folk, and all the while no line was wrung
> In praise or balm of aught from my frost-bitten tongue
> . . . . . . . .
> Then I walked in a room where Irish poets were. . . .
> (*On These* 141)

After spending time with the Irish poets, the speaker falls into a regenerative slumber.

While Locke had spoken "[w]ithout pretense to [its] political significance," others such as Marcus Garvey, A. Philip Randolph, and Claude McKay found a great deal of "political significance" in a comparison of African-American and Irish people. Before twenty-five thousand delegates at the 1920 Universal Negro Improvement Association (UNIA) convention in Madison Square Garden, Marcus Garvey began his keynote address by reading a telegram he was sending—not to a famous person of African descent, but to Eamon de Valera, president of the year-old Dáil Éireann, the Irish Parliament. Referring to the ongoing Irish war for independence from England, Garvey read, "We believe Ireland should be free even as Africa shall be free for the Negroes of the world. Keep up the fight for a free Ireland" (Hill 499). The Irish struggle for cultural and political autonomy had inspired the leader of the Back to Africa movement, and Garvey, who had built his movement largely on pageantry, knew a good symbol when he saw one.[8]

Throughout his long life, Garvey's rival W. E. B. Du Bois also frequently compared the black and Irish situations. As he wrote to Arthur P. Kelly in 1953, "[your father] and I were classmates in the class of 1890 at Harvard, and we had certain peculiar interests in common, he being an Irishman, and I a Negro" (qtd. in Weinberg 246). Years earlier, Du Bois had discussed some of these commonalities in a series of articles in the *Crisis*. In January 1920 he wrote that "England has sinned against dependent and backward people to an unbelievable extent" and urged independence for Ireland and England's African colonies, lest the "up-striving and embittered darker races of the whole earth" rise up against their oppressor (108). When readers remonstrated with Du Bois for criticizing England, noted for its early abolition of slavery and suppression of the slave trade, and allying himself with Ireland, ancestral home of the many racist Irish Americans, he replied in the March issue, "we who suffer in slavery and degradation,—shall we hesitate to extend a hand of sympathy to the Irish, simply because their descendants in America are so largely the followers of American snobbery?" (238).

A. Philip Randolph, editor of the radical black journal *The Messenger,* also compared the Irish political situation to that of his own people, though his goal was to convert African Americans to socialism. In the summer of 1919, as racial violence flared in America and many blacks took up the banner of the New Negro, Randolph exhorted them to follow the revolutionary activities occurring worldwide. In an article entitled "A New Crowd—A New Negro," he stated, "The Seine Feiners [*sic*] are the New Crowd in Ireland fighting for self-determination" (19). Old Crowds around the world he likened to appendixes, useless and potentially harmful. Garvey, Du Bois, and Randolph all made use of the Irish struggle for independence, but, though it succeeded where they did not, its outcome was not entirely positive. The Irish Free State had a repressive and isolationist government that practiced extreme forms of censorship and chose not to side with the Allies in World War II because it did not wish to help England. Though inspirational, Ireland for the Irish became as problematic as Africa for the Africans.

The writer and socialist Claude McKay seems to have had a special affinity for the Irish Renaissance and Irish politics, although he knew of and was sympathetic to many cultural and political movements. During the summer of 1920, he wore a green necktie to a Sinn Fein demonstration in London and was addressed with camaraderie as "Black Murphy" and "Black Irish." Back in America a year later, McKay wrote an article entitled "How Black Sees Green and Red" for the radical journal *Liberator*. In this piece he described the demonstration in London and stated that "[f]or that day at least I was filled with the spirit of Irish nationalism—although I am black!" (58). McKay felt that his position as a colonial subject and his peasant roots helped him understand Irish people better than the English government, the English socialists, or those whom he termed the "anglicized Irish" like George Bernard Shaw (60). He described his empathy for the Irish people as one based in their common "peasant's passion for the soil" (59).[9]

McKay's relation to Irish people and the cause of Irish independence illustrates not only the possibilities but also the dangers of this type of ethnic comparison. His reference to the "peasant's passion for the soil" is a vague and troublesome notion of similarity. The primitivist mindset of the times, which affected both whites and blacks, played a role in making ethnic comparisons available, often creating spurious similarities between disempowered groups. Many believed, for example, that nonwhite peoples and certain white ethnic groups like the Irish were emotional, sensual, and childlike. One might think of Torrence's reference to Irish drama as "vital . . . and charming" ("The New Negro Theatre" 80). Despite the problematic aspects of these comparisons, it is good, in this age of self-segregation, to see marginalized groups reaching out to each other.

### Black America in Irish Minds

Although black on Irish literary influence was nearly nonexistent at the turn of the century, references to African Americans appear occasionally in the writings of Irish Renaissance leaders W. B. Yeats and Lady Gregory. In the 1905 edition of the Abbey publication *Samhain,* Yeats complained about the harsh reception of the company's plays in Ireland. Searching for a way to explain this phenomenon, he suggested that the

Irish people's loss of self-confidence, which he connected to the decline of the Irish language, caused their reluctance to accept humorous, imaginative, or critical presentations of Irish life. "If Ireland had not lost the Gaelic," he wrote, "she never would have had this sensitiveness as of a *parvenu* when presented at Court for the first time, or of a negro newspaper" (*Explorations* 192). Yeats's correlation of the "sensitiveness" of Irish nationalists and African-American journalists was accurate: apparently the latter's outspoken condemnation of negative coverage in the mainstream press was known across the Atlantic as well as in America.

Lady Gregory experienced several connections between black and Irish culture while touring America with the Abbey Theatre in 1911. For instance, when the company arrived in Providence, Rhode Island, in October of that year, they found a petition against *The Playboy of the Western World* waiting for them at the Police Commissioners' office. Lady Gregory recorded in *Our Irish Theatre* that after she had successfully responded to accusations of obscenity and misrepresentation and ensured that the play would be produced, "[t]he police people said that they had had the same trouble about a negro play said to misrepresent people of colour" (185). The officers may have been thinking of *The Clansman,* an adaptation of Thomas Dixon's popular 1905 novel which asserted white superiority. *New York Age* drama critic Lester Walton noted that the play was protested by African Americans in Camden, New Jersey, late in 1909, and since black characters figured in so few plays at the time, *The Clansman* may well have been the one protested in Providence two years later ("Theatrical Comment").

Lady Gregory continued her train of thought from Lowell, Massachusetts, remarking the "sensitiveness" of the various ethnic groups who had managed to require police reports not to disclose the nation of origin of those charged with crimes (186). Her attitude parallels Yeats's on "negro newspapers"—interested, but not altogether sympathetic since she felt excess "sensitiveness" produced the mobs who disrupted plays at the Abbey. Because they encountered African Americans reacting to prejudice rather than as fellow artists, Yeats and Lady Gregory understandably associated them with the overzealous nationalists of their own country.

When black writers came in contact with people of Irish descent, the results were quite different. Claude McKay appears to have been quite successful at gaining Irish and Irish-American sympathy. In addition to the warm reception at the 1920 Sinn Fein rally described in his essay "How Black Sees Green and Red," he recorded two incidents in his autobiography, *A Long Way from Home,* in which Irish Americans made a connection between his racial situation and Ireland's (post)colonial status. In the winter of 1921, shortly after returning from London, he visited his old mentor Frank Harris, editor of *Pearson's Magazine.* McKay brought along a copy of his first publication outside Jamaica, *Spring in New Hampshire.* Harris congratulated him on publishing in London but then grew angry when he realized that McKay had left his militant poem "If We Must Die" out of the book on the advice of his publishers. McKay described Harris's reaction as follows: "'You are a bloody traitor to your race, sir!' Frank Harris shouted. 'A damned traitor to your own integrity. That's what the English and civilization have done to your people. . . . The English make obscene sycophants of their subject peoples. I am Irish and I know. But we Irish have guts the English cannot rip out of us. I'm ashamed of you, sir'" (98). Harris's harsh words sparked a change of mind in McKay about omitting "If We Must Die" and several other powerful poems, and McKay resolved to include them in his forthcoming American publication, *Harlem Shadows.* Harris had been able to give him this advice, McKay believed, because he was also a member of one of England's "subject peoples" and therefore understood McKay's situation.

Several years later, McKay was once again helped by an Irish American who he felt made a connection between racial and colonial oppression. During the spring and summer of 1926, McKay worked for the Irish-American movie director Rex Ingram in France. Ingram wrote poetry, shared many of McKay's radical opinions, and was an informed conversationalist on "the life and thought and achievements of minority groups" (274). His friendliness with McKay, which extended to inviting him to dine at his private table, incurred the wrath of many of the American film crew and of one Italian who had lived in America and acquired its prejudices. The Italian man goaded McKay until he pulled a knife and chased him around a bus. When his anger faded, McKay realized that he had just enacted the stereotype of the knife-wielding Negro, and he was certain that he had lost his job. Although another employee played up the stereotype to Ingram in an attempt to get McKay fired, Ingram refused even to chastise McKay, and, when the movie season was over, he gave him a train ticket and 600 francs. McKay did not record Ingram's explanation for his open-minded and generous actions, writing simply, "Rex Ingram's face revealed that he possessed an intuitive understanding of poets. He is Irish" (276). For the primitivist McKay, who believed in the poetic nature of the Irish people, that was all that needed to be said. However, Ingram's motivation is, at bottom, unknown, despite McKay's assertions. McKay recorded more black-Irish connections than anyone, but it is unclear how many of them were real.

Because Yeats and Lady Gregory did not meet African-American writers like McKay and they knew little of American racial politics, they were less sympathetic to black people than the Irish Americans McKay encountered. Indeed, it would have been difficult for Irish people to have made black-Irish comparisons equally often, for not only did the Irish Renaissance predate the movement in Harlem, but while America enjoyed the Abbey Theatre's tours, the corresponding black entertainment in Ireland consisted of "funny nigger comics" in the 1880s and "nine real American negroes" a generation later—that is, minstrel shows (J. O'Brien 47). A deeper understanding of African-American culture and its relevance to the situation in Ireland would have to wait for the struggle for Catholic civil rights in Northern Ireland in the 1960s and 70s. However, despite the frequent lack of information and interaction, Irish and Irish-American people in the early twentieth century often made explicit connections to their own experiences when assessing African-American actions. Although, like the others discussed in this chapter, these comparisons were sometimes rooted in stereotypes, the inspiration they gave to the writers suggests the usefulness of cross-cultural study and the limitations of investigating only intraracial literary interaction.

# 1

# Waking from the Nightmare

## The Origins of Renaissance

In other countries the past is the neutral ground of the scholar
and the antiquary; with us it is the battlefield.
*Member of the Young Ireland movement*

If you know your history, then you would know
where you're coming from.
*Bob Marley*

To understand why comparisons between African Americans and Irish
people were made so frequently in the early part of this century, it is
necessary to examine their histories. These two groups have in common a
strong sense of a powerful, violent past, exemplifying James Clifford's
assertion that "[t]hroughout the world indigenous populations have had
to reckon with the forces of 'progress' and 'national' unification. The
results have been both destructive and inventive. Many traditions, languages, cosmologies, and values are lost, some literally murdered; but
much has simultaneously been invented and revived in complex, opposi-
tional contexts" (16). The histories of African Americans and Irish
people alike show both the destruction and the invention described by
Clifford.

### A History of Conquest

When the Anglo-Normans came to Ireland in the twelfth century, they
encountered not a united nation under one ruler but a patchwork of

small tribal land divisions united under several provincial kings, whose inhabitants fought each other as often as they fought the English. Indeed, one dispossessed Irish leader, Diarmait Mac Murchada (Dermot MacMurrough) invited the Anglo-Normans into the country, hoping to ally himself with them and regain his lands (Martin 44). By 1250, the Anglo-Normans controlled two-thirds of the island. After the mid-thirteenth century, however, Irish culture experienced a revival as many of the descendants of the Norman settlers assimilated to Irish customs and adopted the Irish language and others died in the Black Death of 1348. The area under English control shrank over time until in 1494 it totaled only about 60 square miles around Dublin on the eastern coast.

The rulers of England were deeply concerned about the acculturation of their vassals in Ireland. Beginning in 1297, a series of laws was passed which attempted to separate loyal subjects from "degenerate" subjects and "Irish enemies." This legislation culminated in the Statutes of Kilkenny of 1366 in which England attempted to strengthen its position in Ireland through cultural segregation: subjects of the crown were forbidden Irish law, language, sports, and spouses. Bards and minstrels were outlawed as spies. Although the Statutes of Kilkenny were ignored as often as they were enforced, they indicated English distress over the state of affairs in Ireland, and they foreshadowed the more severe measures of the centuries to come (E. Curtis 112–14).

During the sixteenth century, Henry VIII and Elizabeth I, who paid more attention to Ireland than their predecessors, found it necessary to effectively reconquer the land, subduing first the Norman-Irish and then the native Irish people. Following a policy known as plantation, they encouraged English and Scottish Protestants to settle in Ireland and made choice lands available to them by dispossessing the native Catholic Irish landowners.[1] Partly by virtue of numbers, some plantations succeeded where earlier attempts to control the culture and language of Ireland had failed. With the new inhabitants came schools that did not teach in Irish and courts where Irish speakers would require an interpreter: the Tudor monarchs and their advisors understood the importance of language to political domination and national identity (Beckett 37).[2] Edmund Spenser, who served in the retinue of the Lord Deputy of Ireland, wrote that "the wordes are the Image of the minde So as they procedinge from the minde the mynd must be nedes affected with the wordes So that the speache beinge Irishe the harte muste nedes be Irishe for out of the abundance of the harte the tonge speakethe" (119).[3] Oliver Cromwell brutally intensified the practice of plantation initiated by his predecessors, and his successors completed the conquest of Ireland, crushing the Irish at the end of the seventeenth century so badly that they did not mount another rebellion for a hundred years.

While the Irish were deprived of their distinctive language and culture without leaving their island home, enslaved Africans experienced a similar loss when communication and culture were disrupted both intentionally and incidentally by the slave trade. The geography of sub-Saharan Africa had caused cultures to develop in small, isolated groups and had facilitated the evolution of more than eight hundred languages and dialects; because Africans with a common language were often separated upon capture, on the slave ships, or upon being sold, the possibility of retaining one's native tongue during slavery was limited (Sowell 184; Thompson 162).[4]

The Atlantic slave trade transported approximately 11.5 million Africans between the mid-fifteenth and mid-nineteenth centuries. The majority of those who were brought to what is now the United States came from the coastal and interior areas of west and west-central Africa. Even so, they spoke many different tongues and practiced customs sometimes as divergent from each other's as from the American colonists'. After 1720, 80 percent of new slaves arrived in the American colonies directly from Africa rather than from other slave-owning parts of the Western Hemisphere. Owners often preferred these new slaves, termed "outlandish," to the acculturated "seasoned" slaves who were more expensive, had often been discarded by island plantations, and were likely to foment rebellion (D. Wright 17, 9, 12, 20).

New slaves were taught English (or French, or Spanish), instructed in their owners' expectations, and generally introduced to the new country by seasoned slaves or by white servants. The rate of acculturation varied, depending on the amount of time spent with non-slaves, the level of urban development in the area, the number of "outlandish" slaves present, and the degree of supervision. Among the slowest to acculturate were the rural coastal slaves of South Carolina and Georgia who worked independently in rice fields cultivated with African technology. Their culture retained many African elements and their blend of English and central African languages, known as Gullah or Geechee, survives today (D. Wright 89, 83).

**Legalized Oppression**

Once conquered or enslaved, both Irish people and African Americans suffered under an oppressive system. Theodore Allen details the similarities in *The Invention of the White Race:* neither people had the most basic human rights, as the law "destroyed the original forms of social identity, and then excluded the oppressed groups from admittance into the forms of social identity normal to the colonizing power" (82).

The law was used in Ireland to keep the Catholic majority down. In the late seventeenth century, the Catholic Irish attempted to throw off English rule by backing James II, the last Catholic ruler of England. Their forces suffered a series of defeats at the hands of William III's commanders, leading to the Treaty of Limerick in 1691. This treaty, designed mainly to confiscate the property of large estate owners, was lenient and loosely written, but the writers of the treaty would not be ruling Ireland. Faced with the daunting prospect of governing a large rebellious population, the Protestant elite controlling the country took advantage of the treaty's loopholes and passed a series of harsh statutes known as the Penal Laws.[5]

These laws were, in effect, a three-pronged effort to render Catholics powerless: first, their religious practices were severely restricted; second, their secular rights were removed; and third, they were heavily taxed. The Penal Laws exiled all bishops and required priests to register with the government. Catholics could not legally vote or intermarry, own guns or good horses, become lawyers or soldiers, or hold political office. Education and property rights were severely restricted as well. Rents to the landlords and tithes to the Protestant Church of Ireland were fixed and inflexible, regardless of one's actual income or religious affiliation. Several times during the seventeenth century, Irish people were sold to other countries as soldiers or plantation laborers (Allen 73–74).

The Penal Laws were, however, not entirely successful: although they were extremely harsh on paper, they were generally enforced loosely and sporadically. The Irish Parliament succeeded in confiscating land, and thus political power, from Catholic people, but hedge schools and secret masses were organized to fight the educational and religious restrictions. Many landowners converted to Protestantism solely to keep their lands and remained friendly to their Catholic neighbors, and historian R. F. Foster notes that more conversions to Protestantism occurred *after* the laws began to be repealed in the late eighteenth century than before (206). Although the Catholic Irish population was crushed politically in one sense, with no representation in parliament and no rebellions from 1690 to 1798, many middle-class urban Catholics prospered in the available professions as merchants, moneylenders, and doctors. Manifesting considerable economic power, they and the English pressured the Irish Parliament to initiate repeal of the Penal Laws in 1778. These statutes' most lasting effects were Protestant contempt and fear, and Catholic servility, resentment, and suspicion—primarily psychological and spiritual effects, yet extremely damaging ones (Foster 205, 220, 207). The repeal of the Penal Laws in the late eighteenth century and the completion of Catholic emancipation in the early nineteenth century brought hopes of a new day in Ireland, much as the Emancipation Proclamation and the ratification of the antislavery amendments would in America. However, in the mid-nineteenth century the suffering of the Irish continued, with both political and natural causes. A series of crop failures culminated in the Potato Famine of 1845–49, in which approximately one million people died and several million more were compelled to emigrate (Foster 324).

   In America, oppression was legalized both during and after slavery. The nearly four million American slaves enumerated in the 1860 census had no right to be educated, own property, marry, maintain a family, vote, or choose an occupation. It was a crime to give a slave a Bible, but not to rape one. Although somewhat protected by their status as valuable property, slaves were completely subject to the caprice of their owners. They were prevented from escaping by a system designed to foster dependence and ignorance: most owners provided food, clothing, housing, and daily schedules and forbade any education. Field slaves worked from dawn to dusk and then had to do their personal chores, such as cooking. The most common offense was "impudence," which had an extremely broad definition. The five hundred thousand free African Americans listed in the 1860 census were mostly poor, unskilled, and devoid of legal protection or civil rights, but they were often literate and acculturated to urban living (Bennett 87, 94–95; Sowell 187, 195–96).

   After the ratification of the 13th, 14th, and 15th Amendments in the late 1860s, African Americans were technically full citizens of the United States. However, the Reconstruction, in which Northern troops enforced the principles of equality, lasted only twelve years. For most, conditions changed little from slavery to freedom. Sharecropping and strict work laws often replaced slavery, with former slaves incurring astronomical debts—often purposely inflated—that bound them to a creditor as surely as to an owner. Disgruntled whites organized vigilante groups like the Ku Klux Klan in order to keep blacks submissive, and lynching, which had not originated as a race-specific practice, increasingly happened principally to African Americans. One notable change involved married black women increasingly staying home with their children, distressing whites who had previously relied on them for domestic labor.

Beginning in the 1880s, Jim Crow laws were passed in the South to prevent interracial social contact, especially eating and marriage, and to keep the African-American population in its place (Bennett 256–57). Skirting the 14th and 15th Amendments, laws created segregated jobs, neighborhoods, restaurants, and transportation. Black voting became a brief memory of the Reconstruction. In Birmingham, Alabama, blacks and whites could not legally play checkers together (Bennett 268). The Supreme Court's decision in *Plessy* v. *Ferguson* (1896) institutionalized "separate but equal" treatment of and facilities for African Americans across the nation, which in practice rarely meant equal and quite frequently meant nonexistent. Education, for example, was difficult to find in the South, especially beyond the elementary level and in rural areas: those who could afford to turned to private education, and those who could not often went without. Atlanta did not have a public high school for African Americans until 1924 (Sowell 202–4).

### A Digression Concerning the Anglo-Irish

Although to this point I have focussed on the Catholic population of Ireland, in order to discuss the Irish Renaissance one must address the complex situation of the Anglo-Irish. This group, composed of gentry, professional, mercantile, and working classes, filled the gaps in Irish politics and society caused by the enforcement of the Penal Laws. Over the years, however, they came to find that their loyalty to England was not always rewarded: the English government viewed Ireland with its own ends in mind. Yet because of their fear of Catholic power, the Anglo-Irish almost always supported legislation enforcing discrimination against Catholics. They felt trapped between English machinations and the desires of the disempowered Catholic majority.

Although the term was not coined until the late 1700s, the eighteenth century was the heyday of the Anglo-Irish Ascendancy, the power elite made up of landed aristocrats, influential professionals, and high-rank-ing civil servants. Membership in this group was not restricted on the basis of birth or ethnic origin, but by religion. Of the twenty-five percent of Ireland's population that was Protestant, only that half who were Anglicans could belong to the Ascendancy. Few barriers existed beyond this one: the descendants of acculturated Normans rubbed elbows with the grandchildren of Cromwellian settlers, and the sons of blacksmiths, lawyers, and country gentry met at Trinity College, where they aspired to serve in the Irish Parliament (Foster 173). As the years passed, an Anglo-Irish consciousness developed, particularly among the Ascendancy, and the sense of marginalization from English affairs and isolation within Ireland deepened. Many resented their dependence on England and feared it would lead to betrayal; they began to speak of freedom for Ireland but were, as yet, unwilling to include the Catholics in their inchoate vision.

As the eighteenth century progressed, Anglo-Irish people increasingly demonstrated their concern with identity. They began to call themselves "Irish gentlemen" rather than "the Protestants of Ireland" or "the English of this kingdom" (Foster 178). They developed a passion for building so great it often surpassed the capacity of their purses, and they memorialized themselves and their possessions in innumerable portraits and landscapes. In 1785, the Irish Academy (afterward the Royal Irish Academy) for the study of Irish history and achievements was founded. The last two decades of the century brought the beginnings of Catholic emancipation and the Act of Union, both of which most Anglo-Irish people had strongly opposed. The Act of Union took away much of their political power by dissolving the Irish Parliament. In the future, laws governing Ireland would be made at Westminster, and no guarantee existed that the Irish representatives would be Anglo-Irish.

The Act of Union signaled the beginning of the decline of the Anglo-Irish. By the middle of the nineteenth century, many were supporting the Union their parents had rejected because the alternative had become Home Rule with a widely enfranchised Catholic majority. The dream of an Ascendancy-led Ireland was fast fading as tenants declined to vote for landowners' preferred candidates and began to join proto-nationalist organizations. Many Anglo-Irish people saw the Union as their economic and physical protection, but as the century closed, they were not at all certain that it would last. The means by which they had defined their identity began to collapse as well: their great tracts of land were increasingly split up and their elaborate Dublin townhouses were often converted into tenement housing.

The disintegration of their identity and political power made a sizable number of Anglo-Irish people begin to visualize an independent Ireland whose sectarian rifts could be closed. Like many in the Catholic majority, they felt abused by England, and their resentment provided a fruitful nexus for Protestant and Catholic nationalists. The Young Ireland movement, the Parliamentary party, and the Irish Republican Brotherhood (IRB) all had Anglo-Irish members and even leaders, including Thomas Davis, John Mitchel, and Charles Stewart Parnell. Indeed, the Gaelic League, like the Young Ireland movement, was founded with the intention of uniting members of different faiths who cared about Ireland and Irish culture.

Because the Anglo-Irish elite lived in "the big house," their Catholic Irish tenants called them "master," and words like "plantation" crop up in discussions of Anglo-Irish history, some draw parallels between them and the slaveowners of the South. However, the comparison is limited at best. Southern slaveowners did not ally themselves with the black population out of resentment against a distant central government, though they certainly rebelled against its policies and tried to convince their slaves that they were in the right. A better parallel might be between the free blacks and the slaves of the nineteenth century. In many cases, freedmen and women did not readily identify with their enslaved cousins, and in some cases, they even owned them as slaves. When the emancipated slaves and their descendants began to move North, much of the long-standing free black population was dismayed by the arrival of their unwashed kin. However, this attitude was not widespread long into the twentieth century.

### Hegemonic Views

In the years before the Harlem and Irish renaissances, the majority of English and Anglo-Irish people and white Americans perceived Catholic Irish people and black Americans in similar ways. The work of John Beddoe and Thomas Nast, discussed previously, is typical of the attitudes in both popular and high culture, which characterized African Americans and Irish people as physically and mentally inferior to the respective dominant cultures. In the case of African Americans, a belief among many whites in "the fundamental identity of complexion, character, and intellectual capacity" acted to their detriment (Gates, *Figures* 18). They were often considered most closely related to apes and were believed to be incapable of complex thought or sophisticated written expression.

African Americans were thought to be an emotional and sensual race, prone to dissipation and unendowed with the capacity for moral or aesthetic judgment. Most whites felt either that African Americans had been degraded by slavery, or that by nature they were fit only for servitude. In either case, after emancipation black people were faced with the necessity of proving their humanity and equality.

The nature of stereotypes suggests that considerable overlap would occur between hegemonic views of African Americans and of Irish people. Indeed, both groups were frequently characterized as simple and superstitious folk endowed with a potential for violence, which was emphasized as they fought for civil rights. Many also regarded them as lazy and dirty peasants lacking the capacity for self-regulation or independence. Like animals or children, they were believed to be unconcerned with the past or the future. As Nast's illustration indicates, African Americans and Irish people were not only perceived similarly, but compared to one another.

The dominant cultures profited psychologically and materially from their attitudes toward their subject peoples. Because of this profit, they would relinquish neither the stereotypes nor their control over the institutions that produced them without a struggle. Thus, Lady Gregory's London publisher initially asked her to rewrite her rendition of ancient Irish sagas, *Cuchulain of Muirthemne,* on a more juvenile level (*Seventy Years* 399). Although the publisher may have seen this simply as a marketing strategy, Lady Gregory was indignant. Recalling similar feelings, Jessie Fauset told an interviewer in 1932 that her first novel, *There Is Confusion,* was originally rejected because it depicted sophisticated, bourgeois black people (Sylvander 73). As Edward Said wrote of a similar stereotype, Orientalism, it "is not an airy European fantasy about the Orient, but a created body of theory and practice in which, for many generations, there has been a considerable material investment" (6). Hegemonic representations of African Americans and Irish people were generated from a potent social force.

### Great Migrations

Geographical issues played a large part in the experiences of Irish people and African Americans that engendered the Irish and Harlem renaissances. The Irish not only emigrated from Ireland but also moved from the poverty and famine-stricken Irish countryside to the cities, while African Americans began to move north. Massive Irish immigration to the cities and to other countries in the nineteenth century threatened the rural folk culture, and the Irish Renaissance might be said to be a response to that threat, an attempt at preservation. However, the mostly Anglo-Irish intellectuals who began to collect and study Irish sagas and folklore were motivated as much by a pan-European interest in studying the past as by an Irish desire to preserve a culture laid waste by famine and emigration. Indeed, a movement impelled by cultural decline alone would likely have begun many years previously, for while the Potato Famine of 1845–49 had a tremendous impact on Irish life, emigration had been steady for years before this particular potato blight struck. People were already leaving at a rate of 130,000 per year in 1841, and mass emigration continued until the population of Ireland was down to 4,400,000 in 1911, nearly halved from 8,200,000 before the Famine (Foster 323–24). Conditions were so wretched even before the 1840s that African-American slaves in the United States had a longer life expectancy, better living quarters, and better nourishment than the average Irish peasant, for though they were not free, they were at least considered valuable property (Sowell 18).[6]

While dramatic population changes influenced the Irish Renaissance, the connection was stronger and more direct in the case of the Harlem Renaissance. In the late nineteenth century, Harlem was a white upper-middle-class neighborhood in the midst of a building boom. Washington, D.C., was the capital of black culture, as many political organizations, wealthy families, and writers made their homes there; however, as late as 1910, 75 percent of African Americans were rural dwellers, and 90 percent lived in the South (Wintz 17, 13). The first black people in Harlem were, ironically, middle-class New Yorkers moving away from the Irish on the middle West side (Sowell 38).

Beginning around 1915, a combination of attractions in the North and deterrents in the South caused African Americans to move slowly but steadily north. As economic conditions worsened in the South because of boll weevils, flooding, and rising food prices, word spread of better times in the North, where the war had virtually eliminated European immigration, a major source of factory labor, while stimulating industrial growth. Fear of violence also impelled northward migration: lynching increased after the United States entered World War I, and race riots gave the summer of 1919 the epithet "Red Summer." Given these conditions, many African-American leaders abandoned the idea of the South as home and future and focussed instead on the growing northern communities (Wintz 14–16, 13, 6). As Thomas Sowell phrases it, "More than three-quarters of a million blacks left the South in the decade of the 1920s—more people than migrated from Ireland to the United States during the famine decade of the 1840s" (209).[7]

Areas like Harlem offered opportunity: one could leave southern, rural, and familial restrictions behind and come to a place where colorful success stories were told, like that of Pig Foot Mary, who parlayed her makeshift food stand into a small fortune in real estate (Lewis 109–10). These feelings were eloquently described as early as 1902 by Paul Laurence Dunbar, who wrote in his novel *Sport of the Gods* that immigrants from the South "had heard of New York as a place vague and far away, a city, that, like Heaven, to them had existed by faith alone. All the days of their lives they had heard of it, and it seemed to them the centre of all the glory, all the wealth, and all the freedom of the world" (68). If anything, this sentiment only grew over time.

## A New Spirit

Although material conditions were poor in Ireland and in Harlem during the renaissances, some improvement had occurred since the days of legalized oppression under slavery and the Penal Laws. The Famine and the failure of Reconstruction had been great setbacks, entrenching poverty in Ireland and discrimination in America, but a new spirit was coming to both peoples.

With the abolition of the Penal Laws and with full Catholic emancipation in 1829, many Catholics had taken up parliamentary and revolutionary agitation, although the majority of the population was concerned mainly with local and agrarian issues—that is, when they had enough to eat. By the late nineteenth century, Catholic political figures had been joined by a number of Protestants disillusioned with England and eager to repeal the Act of Union and acquire Home Rule for Ireland. Leading the Home Rulers of the Irish Parliamentary party was "The Chief," Charles Stewart Parnell, whose political collapse and subsequent death following the exposure of his relationship with Mrs. Katharine O'Shea scarred the nation. Yeats stated in a lecture delivered to the Royal Academy in Sweden on the occasion of his 1923 Nobel Prize that "[t]he modern literature of Ireland, and indeed all that stir of thought which prepared for the Anglo-Irish war, began when Parnell fell from power in 1891. A disillusioned and embittered Ireland turned from parliamentary politics; an event was conceived; and the race began, as I think, to be troubled by that event's long gestation" (*Autobiographies* 559).

Many scholars have followed Yeats in stating that political activism gave way to cultural nationalism in the years between the death of Parnell and the 1916 Easter Rising.[8] Foster's recent study of modern Ireland argues otherwise: citing the growth of such political organizations as the United Irish League, the Ancient Order of Hibernians, and the Irish labor movement, he posits cultural nationalism as the province of a tiny minority that existed alongside thriving popular political organizations (431–33). The average Irish person at the turn of the century was an agrarianist more than a nationalist, and when a nationalist, one in the tradition of the Young Ireland movement of a generation past, not that of the Irish Renaissance (Foster 459). However, like their counterparts in black America a generation later, the Irish were being reborn.

Although most cultural nationalist organizations were tiny and did not affect large numbers of people, two bear mentioning, the Gaelic Athletic Association (GAA) and the Gaelic League. The GAA, described by Foster as a "powerful rural network" dedicated to reviving Irish sports and suppressing English ones, was founded by Michael Cusack in Tipperary in 1884 (447). In addition to popularizing hurling and Gaelic football, the GAA drew a connection between rejecting English games and rejecting the rest of English culture. It was never only a sports movement, for it also sponsored periodicals, publishing poetry by Yeats, among others, and many members of the revolutionary organization the Irish Republican Brotherhood (IRB) also belonged to the GAA (Lyons 39–40; Foster 454). Because of its rural and popular nature, the GAA was one of the largest cultural nationalist organizations.

The Gaelic League, whose goal was to revive the Irish language, was founded nine years later in 1893 by Eoin MacNeill and Douglas Hyde. The League was originally intended to bring Protestants and Catholics together, and its membership also crossed class lines, making it a heterogeneous organization for its time. Many Catholic Gaelic Leaguers linked Gaelicness to Catholicism, however, leading the Protestant membership to dwindle after 1900 (Lyons 43). The League was an extremely small organization until the turn of the century, when the Boer War galvanized anti-English sentiment and boosted its membership. Although small, the Gaelic League included among its members many of the militant nationalists of the first two decades of the twentieth century in Ireland, including Patrick Pearse, leader of the 1916 Easter Rising, Arthur Griffith, founder of the radical organization Sinn Fein, and Eamon de Valera, first president of the revolutionary Republic. Ironically, the Gaelic League was originally a fairly apolitical organization: until the IRB infiltrated it between 1905 and 1910, it was dedicated to achieving cultural autonomy, and many of its members considered political independence an unnecessary or unrealizable end (Foster 450).

In America, similarly dramatic sociopolitical changes were occurring, for World War I was a turning point in the self-image of many African Americans. As Nathan Huggins explains, "World War I had been a kind of puberty rite for peoples the world over. Self-determination, an aim of the Allies in the war, became a slogan in the 1920s. Black intellectuals saw in the Yugoslavs, Czechs, and Irish a clue for their own emancipation and uplift. They, too, were a people to be defined" (*Harlem* 83). Lynching and other forms of racial violence increased after the war as many white Americans attempted to maintain the status quo, but African Americans, armed with the concept of self-determination, began to resist, both physically and psychologically. During violence in Chicago, Longview, Texas, and Washington, D.C., in 1919, African Americans fought back with guns (Lewis 18–20). Radical journals like the *Messenger* became more "bellicose and irreverent," and Marcus Garvey's organization, the Universal Negro Improvement Association (UNIA), prospered by emphasizing racial pride (J. Anderson 119–21). As part of the militant new spirit, Claude McKay wrote the poem "If We Must Die," urging the victims of racial violence to strike back at their oppressors. It concluded: "Like men we'll face the murderous, cowardly pack, / Pressed to the wall, dying, but fighting back!" (*Selected Poems* 36).[9]

Most African Americans were not as radical as McKay, but many were suffused with a new spirit. They were called "New Negroes." This term can be traced at least as far back as an 1895 editorial in the *Cleveland Gazette,* which defined it as "a class of colored people . . . with education, refinement and money" (qtd. in Meier 258). In the thirty years between the *Gazette* editorial and Locke's 1925 publication of the *New Negro* anthology, the term itself was the subject of much debate. Most agreed that New Negroes were self-assured and deserving of respect, not subservient objects of pity. They demanded equal political and social treatment from white Americans, combining elements from the beliefs of several African-American leaders: Du Bois's militancy, Booker T. Washington's self-sufficiency and racial pride, and Marcus Garvey's Pan-

Africanism (Wintz 47). New Negroes were almost never revolutionaries: they were more politically inclined than Locke's largely cultural anthology suggested, but they were not socialists who avidly followed the revolutionary activities of the Russian communists and the Irish nationalists, as A. Phillip Randolph claimed in the *Messenger* (18–19). The vast majority of those who might have identified themselves as New Negroes were demanding only the right to assimilate to American middle-class values, but even this meager claim disturbed the white establishment. As Huggins phrased it, "Apparently white Americans believed in the New Negro as much as black Americans did; he was a threat to one as much as a hope to the other" (*Harlem 56*).

The Harlem and Irish renaissances were partly engendered by similar popular sentiments—popular, at least, among their constituencies—to end physical submissiveness and cultural subordination. Before this spirit took hold, both peoples were largely against the use of physical force to achieve their goals, but gradually more Irish people accepted the idea of fighting for independence and more African Americans practiced self-defense. In both movements, cultural and political activities blended, sharing aims and members.

## New Cultural Centers

With more Irish people and African Americans living in urban areas, centers of cultural and political activity began to take shape. Dublin, and to a lesser extent London, experienced a great deal of Catholic as well as Protestant Irish relocation during the nineteenth century. Once in these cities, those in search of a workable Irish identity and interested in a revival of Irish culture, often Anglo-Irish people, gathered at homes and social clubs and eagerly read the work of Irish scholars and more or less gifted amateurs involved in the pan-European revival of folklore, linguistics, and archaeology (Hunt 11). Influential books included Standish James O'Grady's two-volume set *History of Ireland: The Heroic Period* (1878, 1880), a retelling of Irish heroic legends; Douglas Hyde's *Beside the Fire* (1890) and *Love Songs of Connacht* (1893), collections of stories and poems in Irish and English; Lady Gregory's renditions of ancient sagas, entitled *Cuchulain of Muirthemne* (1902) and *Gods and Fighting Men* (1904); and Yeats's collections of folklore, *Fairy and Folk Tales of the Irish Peasantry* (1888) and *The Celtic Twilight* (1893).

These works were enthusiastically received in urban intellectual circles: Yeats, who had lamented in 1890 that translations of ancient Irish literature were nearly impossible to find, was moved to write in the preface to *Cuchulain of Muirthemne,* "I think this book is the best that has come out of Ireland in my time. Perhaps I should say that it is the best book that has ever come out of Ireland; for the stories which it tells are a chief part of Ireland's gift to the imagination of the world—and it tells them perfectly for the first time" (*New Island* 33; *Explorations* 3). Similarly, John Synge would call this book "still a part of my daily bread" two years after he first read it (qtd. in Gregory, *Theatre* 124).[10] Yeats and Synge were excited because this group of publications was the first modern scholarship to treat Irish sagas and folktales as respectable subjects and to avoid a condescending tone. In the late 1880s, a number of Yeats's early reviews had criticized writers for not treating Irish lore in a more serious fashion: fifteen years later, several works had been published that one could use to connect to an Irish past, and the Irish Renaissance had received a necessary impetus.

A few years later, African Americans of all walks of life were being drawn to Harlem as a burgeoning cultural center. Although the black population of midwestern cities such as Chicago, Detroit, and Cleveland increased more rapidly, New York added the largest number of African Americans to its population in the early twentieth century (Wintz 14). Because of this population increase and the excellent facilities for publishing and artistic performance, New York became the center of African-American literary, political, and social activity, as London and Paris were for Anglophone and Francophone African colonials (Huggins, *Voices* 6). Though many Washingtonians felt disdain for Harlem's "vulgar splendor" and lack of social status or great black universities, by 1920 the headquarters of the NAACP, the Urban League, Marcus Garvey's UNIA, and the emerging literary movement were all situated in Harlem (Wintz 20–22). African-American churches in midtown Manhattan read the signs and followed their parishioners uptown, where clergy like Adam Clayton Powell, Sr., and Reverdy Ransom continued to provide powerful leadership on social and racial issues (J. Anderson 4, 21–24). They were joined by clubs, newspapers, entertainers, professionals, saloons, and criminals (J. Anderson 62). As Cary Wintz puts it, "Harlem . . . was where the action was in black America during the decade following World War I" (22). Other cities had black literary societies and journals, but Harlem had leadership and notoriety.

While African Americans physically moved to Harlem and celebrated it in literature, the Anglo-Irish might be said to have psychologically moved Ireland by focussing on the rural past while living in Dublin or London.[11] Both types of movement created a workable space for a literary renaissance, and both would prove problematic as well. Harlem was an exciting place for African Americans to live in the 1920s, but it was already becoming a slum and a black ghetto. In Ireland, the rejection by many writers of the present and the urban in favor of the past and the rural simplified ignoring the glaring problems of both. Each renaissance city was at once a dream and a nightmare.

## Urban Conditions

Many urban Irish people and African Americans lived in appalling conditions. The history and folklore so popular with urban Anglo-Irish intellectuals dealt almost exclusively with the past or an idealized countryside, but the misery of modern rural Irish life was matched by few places, one of them being Dublin. A 1903 article in the *British Medical Journal* paraphrased the Earl of Dudley, Lord Lieutenant of Ireland: "He had seen the misery of Irish peasants in the West, but nothing comparable with what existed at their own doors in Dublin" ("Housing" 1108). In the early twentieth century, the death rate in the capital reached fifth highest among cities world-wide before it began to decline (Foster 437).

Those who survived spent a good deal of time looking for work, trudging the streets of Dublin, which were so filthy and poorly maintained that they "generated twice as many tons of street sweepings per mile per year as even larger cities such as Edinburgh and Leeds" (J. O'Brien 67). Because of the predominantly non-industrial nature of the city's economy, many working-class people had no skills whatsoever: known as "general laborers," they were forced to depend on the vagaries of temporary employment. They often went home at night to "eighteenth-century tenements bereft of water or sanitation" (Foster 437), as the beautiful townhouses built a hundred and fifty years before by the Anglo-Irish Ascendancy had become warrens for people frequently packed four to a room, or more. In 1885, the average Dublin tenement dwellers lived in one and a half rooms per family. As Joseph O'Brien writes, "inadequate housing and unsanitary accommodation had consigned over one-third of the population to conditions of intolerable overcrowding and, most often, ill health" (23, 126).

Little help could be expected from the city government or the Catholic urban middle class. Despite the former's predominantly nationalist convictions, its members often owned tenements and opposed social programs on political and religious grounds. A 1913 housing inquiry revealed that sixteen of the eighty council members were tenement owners. A resolution forbidding city officials to own tenement property was introduced, but it was ignored (J. O'Brien 152). When the massive Transport Workers' strike threatened participating families with starvation in the same year, the Catholic Church refused to let the children be sent to England, fearing that Protestants would attempt to convert them. Many newspapers, politicians, prominent businesspeople, and city officials joined the Church's condemnation of the fledgling Irish labor movement (Lyons 77). Yeats, preferring labor to what he thought of as the crass capitalism of the Catholic urban middle class, wrote the following lines to describe the latter:

> What need you, being come to sense,
> But fumble in a greasy till
> And add the halfpence to the pence
> And prayer to shivering prayer, until
> You have dried the marrow from the bone;
> For men were born to pray and save:
> Romantic Ireland's dead and gone,
> It's with O'Leary in the grave. (*Poems* 108)

In addition, in an article in the *Irish Worker,* he condemned both the Unionist and nationalist newspapers for inciting citizens against the striking workers (Lyons 78).[12]

Like many Dubliners, Harlemites often lived in squalid conditions. Harlem enjoyed such epithets as "The City of Refuge" and "The Mecca of the New Negro," but Carl Van Vechten also accurately described it in his 1926 novel *Nigger Heaven* (another name for Harlem) as a crowded and dirty ghetto with little egress (45, 149).[13] African-American novelist Wallace Thurman concurred, writing in 1928 that "[t]he people seen on Fifth Avenue [in Harlem] are either sad or nasty looking. The women seem to be drudges or drunkards, the men pugnacious and loud—petty thieves and vicious parasites. The children are pitiful specimens of ugliness and dirt" (qtd. in J. Anderson 144).

Early-twentieth-century migrations by poor southern African Americans occasioned renewed segregation by whites and resentment from African Americans already in residence during the more liberal years at the end of the nineteenth century (Sowell 210–11). Alain Locke proudly reported in his 1925 anthology *The New Negro* that Harlem was "not merely the largest Negro community in the world, but the first concentration in history of so many diverse elements of Negro life" (6). Locke's claims were fairly accurate: in addition to the influx of southerners, West Indians made up one-quarter of Harlem's population during the 1920s because of a migration of 130,000, mainly to New York City, in the first three decades of the century. But relations between the native-born and the immigrants were often strained: many of the former resented the generally superior education, motivation, and business skills of the West Indians, calling them "black Jews" and "monkey-chasers" (Sowell 216, 219). Harlem Renaissance writers made Jamaican-born Marcus Garvey a frequent target of their satire, emphasizing his physical attributes and his love of pomp (Wintz 150, 152).

Probably as a reaction to increased southern and West Indian immigration, the Society of the Sons of New York was founded, with membership limited to wealthy African Americans born in the city (J. Anderson 26). White owners of major Harlem stores maneuvered to avoid integrated hiring, and African Americans often paid white landlords almost twice the rent that white tenants paid elsewhere in Manhattan for comparable quarters (Lewis 108–9). Preachers and journalists encouraged African Americans to open businesses, but customers of their own race were scarce when they did so: many African Americans would patronize white stores and professionals despite their condescension and frequent insults (J. Anderson 66–67). And though Harlem was notorious for its "rent parties," reputed to ooze sex and gin, the purpose of such events was to raise funds to ward off eviction (Lewis 108).

The excitement associated with Dublin and Harlem as urban centers of cultural renaissance often overshadows the desperate poverty with which it coexisted. As Gilbert Osofsky remarked in his 1966 work *Harlem: The Making of A Ghetto,* "[t]he most profound change that Harlem experienced in the 1920's was its emergence as a slum" (135). Dublin's slums, on the other hand, had been growing since the Act of Union of 1800 when the seat of government moved to London and the city lost its economic base. Some Irish historians suggest that Dublin did not even have Harlem's advantage of being situated in a major artistic center: as Joseph O'Brien relates in painful detail, theater, music, painting, libraries, and publishing were all limited. According to him, Dublin's only cultural wealth was its newspapers (44–62). One must therefore take care to balance one's images of the renaissance cities so that they are not, in Hugh Kenner's words, "vivid, credible, and wholly literary" (Foreword viii).

## Political Activity

Despite the crushing poverty, in addition to participating in the cultural activities in Dublin and Harlem, many Irish people and African Americans became involved with the numerous political organizations available to them, which ran the entire spectrum from liberal to radical means of advocating social change.

Irish people enjoyed many political options after Parnell's fall in 1891, including constitutional nationalism, pro-force nationalism, and socialism. On the constitutionalist front, John Redmond replaced Parnell as leader of the Irish Parliamentary party, and he managed to maneuver a Home Rule bill, which would grant a measure of independence, past the House of Commons and the House of Lords by July 1914. This legislation had been debated since the 1870s, and in 1893 had even passed the lower chamber before being dismissed by the Lords. Unfortunately, the beginning of World War I in August 1914 suspended the British Empire's internal political considerations, and Home Rule hung in limbo. Irish people who had followed Redmond and the constitutional nationalists were of two minds at this juncture: a majority (including Redmond) were willing to wait for Home Rule until the war's end, and a radical minority wished to pressure the English into granting it immediately, perhaps by force (Foster 397, 424, 462, 471, 473).

In addition to the frustrating struggle for Home Rule, the Boer War (1899–1902) had also had a radicalizing effect on Irish politics because it offered an opportunity to root against England (Foster 456). In its wake, and that of World War I, tiny and largely inactive organizations such as the Irish Republican Brotherhood (IRB) saw their memberships grow and their energies focus. Redmond's constitutional nationalism appeared ineffective to them and his Irish Parliamentary party the home of fruitless endeavors, for the IRB favored revolution over democratic measures (Foster 474–75).[14] Disciplined and puritanical, this group of Irish-language enthusiasts, romantic revolutionaries, and mystical Catholics preached a message of revolutionary sacrifice: its leaders began to plan their own martyrdom, which they perceived as a cleansing sacrifice that would drive the English and their contaminating influence from the land (Lyons 86). As IRB leader Patrick Pearse wrote in 1915, "[t]he old heart of the earth needs to be warmed with the red wine of the battlefields. Such august homage was never before offered to God as this, the homage of millions of lives given gladly for love of country" (216). The discourse of blood sacrifice was common across Europe before and in the early years of World War I, and even those who did not particularly believe it found it useful for rationalizing and achieving their undertakings (Lyons 91).

One person converted very late in the game to Pearse's camp was the labor leader James Connolly. Connolly and his fellow organizer James Larkin had found socialism slow to catch on in Ireland, a largely unindustrialized country. When Irish people were politicized, it tended to be along agrarian and nationalist lines; they were not often interested in a brotherhood of workers without an Irish national identity in the offing. Dublin trade unions had been growing stronger toward the end of the nineteenth century, but even they frequently rejected Connolly's Irish Socialist Republican party ideals (J. O'Brien 208–9). After the failure of the 1913 strikes, Connolly and the Irish labor movement were gradually absorbed by the nationalist cause. As late as December 1915, Connolly still protested Pearse's rhetoric of blood sacrifice, but in the months that followed, he too joined the preparations for the Easter Rising of 1916, the event that led, indirectly, to Irish independence (Foster 478–79). The trade unionists played an important role in the Rising, and Connolly himself was executed for his participation in it.

Irish people found the renaissance years a time of increased, if not particularly successful, political activity. The downfall of Parnell and the beginning of World War I were stumbling blocks to Home Rule, for which the Irish Parliamentary party had worked so long; the socialists and trade unionists were largely thwarted in their attempts to improve working conditions for Dublin workers; and the Easter Rising would have been a complete failure if the English had not galvanized Irish nationalist sentiment by executing its leaders. In the end, twenty-six of Ireland's thirty-two counties were finally able to form the Irish Free State in 1921.

While African-Americans would not meet with unqualified political success either, increased political activity accompanied the New Negro spirit in Harlem and other African-American communities. As in Ireland, one could choose from a wide range of approaches to change, including the NAACP's racial uplift, Marcus Garvey's Back to Africa program, and the *Messenger*'s socialism.

Speaking of the end of World War I, W. E. B. Du Bois, leader of the NAACP, wrote the following in a 1919 article: "Make way for Democracy! We saved it in France . . . we will save it in the United States of America, or know the reason why" ("Returning" 14). Since its inception in 1909, the NAACP had consistently spurned the accommodationist politics of Booker T. Washington and demanded equal treatment under the law. Even this seemingly moderate position alienated many people of both races who favored Washington's approach. As James Weldon Johnson wryly observed in his autobiography, "Communists, who advocate and work for the overthrow of the entire governmental system, run no such risks as the Negro 'radical' who insists upon the impartial interpretation and administration of existing law" (*Way* 310). Where Washington had been conciliatory, Du Bois refused to hide his thoughts, writing acidic editorials for the *Crisis,* the journal of the NAACP. Du Bois, the NAACP, and Harlem quickly "became identified with the spirit of Negro protest and self-assertion in the minds of the [*Crisis*'s] wide national readership" (Huggins, *Harlem* 21). But the NAACP could not and did not speak to all African Americans. In 1916, Johnson had difficulty convincing the Board of Directors that the organization should be extended to the South, as they feared that southern African Americans would be too conservative (*Way* 314). And its tireless promotion of the black bourgeoisie led West Indian intellectual Hubert Harrison to dub it the "National Association for the Advancement of *Certain* People" in the early 1920s (McKay, *Long Way* 113–14).

Many African Americans displeased with the NAACP turned to Marcus Garvey's UNIA, the only group that appealed to the black urban masses. Garvey began lecturing at the Harlem speakers' corner about "a renascent Mother Africa" in the spring of 1916, and by the end of 1918 he could draw several thousand to rallies at Harlem's Palace Casino. At first, Garvey's references to Africa shocked those who were ashamed or ignorant of their African heritage. No black leader had spoken in this vein since the end of Reconstruction, and the Euro-American vision of "the dark continent" had taken hold in the minds of many people of African descent. For many people, Garvey connected Africa to unity and self-improvement, engendering pride where shame had reigned. As UNIA grew, it attracted black nationalists, socialists, and communists, and it angered Du Bois, the NAACP, and much of the African-American bourgeoisie. When the war ended and racial strife increased, Garvey's organization thrived on the disillusionment prevalent in many African-American communities. But UNIA and Garvey's power collapsed as quickly as they grew: his poor money management incurred the government's wrath in 1922 (though UNIA was already under surveillance by the FBI in 1919) and his courting of the Ku Klux Klan as a fellow separatist organization in the same year inflamed many of his erstwhile supporters. In 1925 Garvey was jailed for mail fraud, and although UNIA continued to exist, its days of glory were over (Lewis 34–44, 111). As Nathan Huggins suggests, the causes of Garvey's success and failure were one and the same: he tried to make his dream of a return to Africa tangible through titles, uniforms, parades, and even an African-American shipping company, and the ranks of his organization swelled accordingly; however, this dream based on expensive and complicated pageantry quickly foundered, as Garvey tried "to produce grand results before he had the experience or organization to manage them" (*Harlem* 43).

The African-American socialists and communists, Garvey's early allies, attracted a much smaller following during the 1920s than the NAACP or UNIA, but they were a vocal minority on the Harlem political scene. These "race radicals" faced a tough challenge when they stood at the speakers' corner at Lenox Avenue and 135th Street: although the average African American was a severely exploited member of the proletariat, he or she was also against immigration and unions and in favor of the capitalist system. Smashed unions and curtailed immigration meant employment opportunities to many African Americans, and their leadership often concurred (Lewis 22). In addition, the arrant racism of most American labor unions did not help them gain African-American sympathy or members. However, during the 1920s, the Communist party made an effort to recruit African Americans and to have its platforms reflect their concerns, advocating interracial socializing and marriage, class struggle as a means to racial equality, and even an African-American state in the Deep South (Wintz 194). But because the American Communist party could not offer viable solutions to racial problems and because it was plagued by racism itself, it was never popular with African Americans: their membership probably peaked at about two hundred out of fifteen thousand total members (Lewis 286).

The era of the Harlem Renaissance opened more political venues to African Americans than it engendered political and social change. Black leaders of the 1920s lacked the power their successors would enjoy: they could not muster the numbers to carry out a successful boycott, and the major political parties cared little about the African-American vote.

Black political figures tended to make speeches on broad issues rather than do battle on the lowest political levels, and this refusal of the majority of African-American leaders to engage in party politics at the level of the ward also hurt their chances for achieving significant changes (Huggins, *Harlem* 31, 26).

In addition to their political activities, many African Americans and Irish people saw literature as a means of social change. The remainder of this work will explore the issues raised by this attitude towards literature: issues of language, identity, and representation.

# 2

# Collaboration, Isolation, and Conflict
## Dilemmas of Language

[E]verything I love has come to me through English; my hatred
tortures me with love, my love with hate.
*W. B. Yeats*

They are ashamed of the past made permanent by the spirituals.
*Jean Toomer*

Language played a key role in the conquest of Ireland and the enslavement of Africans as well as in the cultural renewal of both peoples. Because the dominant cultures had attempted to erase Irish and African-American ancestral languages and then had denigrated their dialects of English, recovering the one and engendering respect for the other were difficult—and in the case of African languages virtually impossible—undertakings. By the time of each renaissance, both the ancestral languages and the dialects of English generated feelings of disdain, shame, and anger in many African Americans and Irish people.

Part of the work of the Harlem and Irish renaissances would be to mitigate the effects of what Paolo Freire calls "cultural invasion" (151) by investing their languages and/or dialects with dignity. In Ireland, the Anglo-Irish writers Douglas Hyde, Lady Gregory, and John Synge developed a literary style that joined Irish syntax and expressions to an English base, creating a distinctive Hiberno-English dialect that they used to translate Irish literature into English and to write their own works. Their efforts showed that serious literature could be written in an Irish dialect of English and helped inspire some of the Harlem Renaissance writers concerned with similar issues.

James Weldon Johnson, like many African-American intellectuals, was looking for an approach "larger than dialect" that would be suitable for high art, and he believed that he had found it in the work of the Irish Renaissance (*American Negro Poetry* xli). Other writers such as Zora Neale Hurston disagreed, resisting Johnson's dichotomy of high and low art, and attempted to create literature using a less-mediated dialect. But even more than Anglo-Irish writers, African Americans lacked access to the cultures and languages of the past. There was no good place to begin to mitigate the bad reputation of black dialects, for the writers could not translate ancient sagas into contemporary dialect and ennoble both forms, as Irish writers had. Both groups found that, unlike many of the nineteenth-century nationalist movements in Europe, they lacked an immediately accessible native language in which to center a cause: those who attempted to substitute English dialects discovered that the long derogation by both dominant and subaltern group members rendered dignifying them extremely difficult (B. Anderson 47).

### Ireland: Ashamed of the Past

As the English gained control over Ireland, Irish gradually declined from an ancient literary and vernacular language that could assimilate newcomers to a disappearing and often despised tongue associated with poverty and illiteracy. Eventually Irish speakers great and small turned against their own language: the nineteenth-century political leader Daniel O'Connell encouraged people to learn English because Irish monolingualism was economically impractical, and many parents and teachers beat children for speaking Irish, trying to force them to use the language of economic opportunity. The National Schools created in 1831 discouraged the use of Irish, and the government refused to assign Irish-speaking teachers to schools in the Gaeltacht, the Irish-speaking part of the country. By 1851 only 28 percent of Irish people informed census-takers that they spoke any Irish at all, down from 33 percent *fluency* fifty years previously (Kenner, *Colder Eye* 63).

The Potato Famine also severely affected the Irish language. The hardest-hit areas of the country were in the west and southwest, where people often farmed only small plots of land for sustenance: these areas were also the heart of the Gaeltacht. By 1901 only 15 percent of the population spoke any Irish at all, and many of those knew only a few words from the classrooms of the Gaelic League.

Paolo Freire has written that "[f]or cultural invasion to succeed, it is essential that those invaded become convinced of their own intrinsic inferiority . . . [and] want to be like the invaders: to walk like them, dress like them, talk like them" (151). By the time of the Irish Renaissance, "cultural invasion" had largely succeeded. Reading matter consisted mainly of English penny dreadfuls and the work of Irish pulp authors like Victor O'Donovan Power, whose characters uttered such Stage Irishisms as "Wisha, faith, 'tis time for us to have a good laugh tonight, imbeersa!" (qtd. in Kenner, *Colder Eye* 70). Cultural arbiters such as John Pentland Mahaffy, Robert Atkinson, and Edward Dowden degraded ancient and contemporary Irish literature, and little children told their siblings to stop speaking Irish to Douglas Hyde, cofounder of the Gaelic League (Hyde, *Language* 161).

The decline of the Irish language dismayed Hyde because he believed, in the nineteenth-century Irish nationalist Thomas Davis's recurrent phrase, that "a nation without a language is a nation without a soul." As Hyde wrote in his 1886 essay "A Plea for the Irish Language," "while our social and commercial relations make it a necessity for every man woman and child in this kingdom to learn English sooner or later, reverence for our past history, regard for the memory of our ancestors, our national honour, and the fear of becoming materialized and losing our best and highest characteristics call upon us imperatively to assist the Irish speaking population at the present crisis" (*Language* 80). Hyde expanded this idea in his essay "The Necessity for De-Anglicising Ireland," first given as a talk for the National Literary Society late in 1892 and taken on the lecture circuit thereafter. He stated that he was not opposed to all things English per se: his concern was that Irish people were adopting the worst aspects of English culture—that is, the most materialist—and discarding their own culture wholesale. Unlike some of his Gaelic League compatriots, Hyde could envision Irish people choosing to keep the English language and the best aspects of English culture, in addition to the Irish language and culture. Most of the Irish Renaissance writers agreed with him.

As Hyde said in his 1905 speech "The Gaelic Revival," "the Irish language . . . is neither Protestant nor Catholic. It is neither a landlord nor a tenant; it is neither a Unionist nor a Separatist" (*Language* 191).

The Gaelic League had been founded by a diverse group of people who hoped to unite the various religious, political, and class factions in Ireland in the name of the Irish language. But as the League grew, the much-hoped-for tolerance did not grow with it. Many of its members hated England with a breathtaking passion, and they advocated a more political role for the League and more extreme positions on issues of language and culture. Hyde was a moderate committed to quiet political change; that is, he preferred "de-Anglicising" to violence or overt political confrontation. He thus tried to serve as a bridge between the League's extremists and those whom they attacked, like the writers of the Irish Renaissance.

On the most basic level, the Gaelic League extremists and the Irish Renaissance came into conflict because the former wanted Irish literature to be in Irish and the latter envisioned an Irish literature that would influence people across Europe. The members of the Irish Renaissance felt that this more cosmopolitan version ought to be in English for purposes of translation and dissemination across the continent, while many Gaelic League members felt that the idea of Irish literature in English was a contradiction in terms and a threat to the League's work. As Patrick Pearse wrote in a letter to the League journal, "[i]f we once admit the Irish literature in English idea, then the language movement is a mistake. Mr. Yeats's precious 'Irish' Literary Theatre may, if it develops, give the Gaelic League more trouble than the Atkinson-Mahaffy combination" (qtd. in M. Murphy 157).[1] Irish Renaissance writers also recognized what the Gaelic League extremists often denied: the Irish language was not spoken widely enough to engender a national much less a cosmopolitan literature. As Yeats phrased it, "[i]f you say a National literature must be in the language of the country, there are many difficulties. Should it be written in the language that your country does speak or the language that it ought to speak?" (*Explorations* 156). In 1977, anticipating literary critics like Homi Bhabha and Houston A. Baker, Jr., Irish poet Seamus Heaney called the English language "not so much an imperial humiliation as a native weapon" (40), but this attitude was not acceptable to many Gaelic League members in Hyde's time.[2]

As both a writer and a member of the Gaelic League, Hyde was well-suited to mediate between these groups. He viewed the work of the Irish Renaissance as a helpful stepping stone to de-Anglicization, not as a betrayal of Irish culture. When the Irish theater movement was inaugurated by the production of Yeats's *Countess Cathleen* and Edward

Martyn's *Heather Field* in 1899, some members of the Gaelic League expressed their displeasure that both plays were in English. Hyde had already discussed with Lady Gregory the possibility of writing and staging plays in Irish, and in August 1900, while visiting her estate, they wrote *Casadh an tSúgáin,* a one-act play based on an Irish folktale. In 1901 it became one of the first plays produced in Irish, with Hyde playing the lead role himself.[3]

Hyde also helped the Irish Renaissance in one way that he had not anticipated. When he collected and translated Irish poetry in *Love Songs of Connacht* (1893), he included literal translations of some of the poems to assist students of Irish who might be confused by the more liberal verse translations. One such passage ran as follows: "And I thought, my storeen, That you were the sun and the moon, And I thought after that, That you were snow on the mouutain [*sic*], And I thought after that, That you were a lamp from God, Or that you were the star of knowledge Going before me and after me" (43). He had not invested a great deal of effort in these study aids, but the result was a simple, direct Hiberno-English much admired by Yeats, who wrote in the 1902 edition of the theater journal *Samhain* that "[t]he prose parts of that book were to me, as they were to many others, the coming of a new power into literature" (*Explorations* 93).

This "new power" had actually revealed itself to Yeats as early as 1888 when Hyde gave him three translated tales for his book *Fairy and Folk Tales.* Hyde's contributions were characterized by a clear and straightforward prose style with occasional Hiberno-English constructions: he avoided attempting to represent an Irish brogue in prose and thus imbued his work with a refreshing seriousness in the minds of many readers. Yeats was extremely pleased with Hyde's efforts, and in 1891, when Hyde translated into English his collection of folktales in Irish, *Leabhar Sgeulaigheachta,* Yeats reviewed it enthusiastically, speaking of Hyde's prose as "that perfect style of his" (*New Island* 49).

In translating *Leabhar Sgeulaigheachta,* Hyde increased his use of Hiberno-English syntax and idiom, convincing Yeats that Hyde would lead Irish writers into the future. But creating a new prose style was not Hyde's primary goal: his books were intended to help people learn Irish and to preserve Ireland's cultural heritage. Thus, the aspect of *Love Songs of Connacht* most impressive to Yeats—the literal translations— was the most marginal aspect to Hyde. Regardless of his intentions, however, Hyde's forays into an Irish-flavored English prose style influenced many of his contemporaries, showing them that Irish prose could escape the derogatory connotations long associated with it.

Lady Gregory and Yeats were displeased that their friend Douglas Hyde's priorities did not jibe with their own. Speaking of her own work, Gregory wrote, "I was the first to use the Irish idiom as it is spoken, with intention and with belief in it" (*Theatre* 124). She acknowledged that Hyde had successfully used "the Irish idiom" before her, but she regretted what she perceived as his lack of commitment to Irish literature, his lack of "intention" and "belief." Like Hyde, Lady Gregory's exposure to Irish and Hiberno-English helped develop her literary style, which she called "Kiltartan" after the area in which she lived. Ann Saddlemyer finds three elements common in Kiltartan: inverted word order ("Putting me down the whole of ye do be"), use of adverbs and adverbial phrases such as "only" or "so," and the "Kiltartan infinitive" ("What business would the people here have but *to be minding* one another's business?") (18). The literary style is a fairly accurate rendering of the local dialect, but it is more densely packed with its characteristic elements than the speech of the local people. Lady Gregory's Kiltartan work included folklore collections, plays, and retellings of ancient sagas, of which the latter have especial bearing on the language issues she addressed: while she used Kiltartan in all of her Irish cultural work, the saga translations were directly inspired by the conflict over the Irish language.

In 1899, a royal commission held an inquiry into the status of the Irish language in the Irish educational system. John Pentland Mahaffy, a Trinity College classicist and an enemy of Hyde, testified that learning Irish would waste students' time, as it was "almost impossible to get hold of a text in Irish which is not religious, or does not suffer from one or the other of the objections referred to," namely, silliness and indecency (qtd. in Stanford and McDowell 104). Mahaffy, who spoke almost no Irish, had based his assertions on the beliefs of his colleague, Robert Atkinson, a philologist, who later testified that all folklore was "at bottom abominable" and that one would be hard pressed to locate an Irish text "in which there is not some passage so silly or indecent as to give you a shock from which you would not recover for the rest of your life" (Stanford and McDowell 108). Hyde countered with a set of testimonials in favor of teaching Irish from leading Celtic scholars in England and on the continent, and an essayist in the Gaelic League's journal, *An Claidheamh Soluis*, managed to call Atkinson's philology credentials into question by demonstrating his ignorance of the Irish verb "to be" (Dunleavy and Dunleavy 210–11).

In the end, the pro-Irish forces won out and the status of Irish in the educational system increased greatly; however, Irish curiosity and sensitivity regarding the old literature also increased. Yeats was invited by the Celtic scholar Alfred Nutt to create a dignified version of the sagas, but he declined, being busy with other work. Lady Gregory took up the project, surprising Yeats, who at first doubted the appropriateness of her background, although his own was no better (Gregory, *Cuchulain* 7). The task was difficult: the sources were in an archaic form of Irish, and the English translations were stultifying and overly literal. In addition, some scholars did not wish the ancient sagas to be popularized because of their questionable moral content: as Yeats wrote in the 1902 edition of *Samhain,* "Mr. Standish O'Grady, who had done more than any other to make us know the old legends, wrote in his *All Ireland Review* that old legends could not be staged without danger of 'banishing the soul of the land.' The old Irish had many wives, for instance, and we had best leave their histories to the vagueness of legend. . . . And so we were to 'leave heroic cycles alone, and not bring them down to the crowd'" (*Explorations* 89). Hence the "indecency" objected to by Mahaffy and Atkinson.

Like Yeats, Lady Gregory disagreed with O'Grady. She felt that accessible translations of the ancient sagas could help reconnect Irish people to their cultural heritage. Taking the Kiltartan dialect from her folklore collections, she worked from 1900 to 1903 and produced two volumes of legends, *Cuchulain of Muirthemne* (1902) and *Gods and Fighting Men* (1904). Her work met with detractors, including Douglas Hyde, who preferred a scholarly to a colloquial translation (Gregory, *Seventy Years* 394). But Lady Gregory rejected translating Irish legends into respectable or juvenile prose, though she intended her work to be a school text, and she created a lucid and energetic version of the Irish sagas. What George Henderson had translated as recently as 1899 as "[y]ou keep me in torment," quoth Cuchulain. "Despatch me quickly; last night, by my troth, I tormented you not. Verily I swear if you torment me, I shall make myself as long as a crane above you" (qtd. in Welch 270), Lady Gregory recast in *Cuchulain of Muirthemne* as "[y]ou are keeping me in torment," said Cuchulain; "put an end to me quickly. For last night," he said, "by my oath, I made no delay with you" (80). She took out details that seemed unnecessary, such as the crane sentence, and smoothed over obscure spots, giving the material a clarity and continuity it had never previously had. Scholarly readers—as well as gifted amateurs like Yeats— were often uncomfortable with these changes, but Lady Gregory replied that she had explained her decisions in the dedication and given all her sources (D. Murphy 8–9).

In recent years, her work has also been criticized for prudish bowdler- izing of the original texts, most notably by Thomas Kinsella, who himself translated some of the same material as *The Tain* in 1969. In his translator's note, Kinsella remarks that Lady Gregory's version "seemed lacking in some important ways, refining away the coarse elements and rationalising the monstrous and gigantesque" (vii). Gregory herself called some of her changes "Bowdlerizing," and her stated goal was to make the legends more acceptable by showing that ancient Irish literature was not crude and barbaric.[4] As she later wrote in her autobiography, "I had done what I wanted: something for the dignity of Ireland. The reviews showed that the enemy could no longer scoff at our literature and its 'want of idealism'" (*Seventy Years* 400).

Kinsella is not, however, particularly objective on this subject. As Joep Leerssen points out, Kinsella added sexual material and created phallic jokes where none existed before, perhaps to distance his work from Lady Gregory's version and to please his own audience (39, 42–43). Where Gregory debarbarized the material, Kinsella emphasized the barbaric and the grotesque, rendering the text exotic. His assessment of her work ignores the fact that she left in some of the material which might well have offended her readers: phallic jokes, partial nudity, and the hero Cuchulain eyeing Emer's breasts.[5]

Both Lady Gregory and Thomas Kinsella saw in the sagas what they wished to see, and not surprisingly: their sources were a collection of fragmented manuscripts, never unitary and often puzzling to a modern reader. Gregory acknowledged that hers was a literary, not a scholarly translation: she wrote in the endnotes to her second book of legends that readers interested in a more rigorous study of the sagas should consult the source texts (*Gods* 462). Her version was the first popular yet fairly accurate rendition of the whole Ulster cycle of tales, and it sold very well.

One of the people influenced by Lady Gregory's adaptation of the sagas was the playwright John Synge. Gregory wrote of Synge that "the rich, abundant speech of the people was a delight to him. When my *Cuchulain of Muirthemme* [*sic*] came out, he said to Mr. Yeats he had been amazed to find in it the dialect he had been trying to master. He wrote to me: 'Your *Cuchulain* is a part of my daily bread'" (*Theatre*

124). Synge was the third member of a trio of Anglo-Irish people who, to differing degrees, learned Irish, immersed themselves in Hiberno-English, and created a new literary style. Late in 1900, Synge published his first translations from Irish to English as part of a review of an edition of Irish poetry. The next summer, during a stay in the Aran Islands where Irish was still common, he continued to translate Irish poetry, and he began to translate some of the islanders' folklore as well as *Oidhe Chloinne Uisnigh,* the legend of Deirdre and Naisi.

As he worked, Synge found that his skill lay in injecting Irish into English, thereby creating "an Irish literature written in English, out of the co-pressure of the two tongues" (Kenner, *Colder Eye* 179), rather than simply translating from Irish into English. Hyde's prose translations in *Love Songs of Connacht* and Lady Gregory's Kiltartan dialect in *Cuchulain of Muirthemne* pointed the way for the younger writer: what Hyde had pioneered and Lady Gregory had refined, Synge made literary. In his work, Irish poetic clichés gained new life, turgid translations caught fire, and new words sprung from the clash of languages. His Hiberno-English was above all fresh, avoiding the banalities of English and Irish traditions.

In addition to its vitality, Synge's Hiberno-English possessed several other characteristics, which Declan Kiberd discusses in his study *Synge and the Irish Language.* First, the differences between English as it was spoken in Ireland and standard English created an interesting tension that Synge manipulated stylistically. For example, in his play *Riders to the Sea,* Nora says of her brother Bartley, "it's destroyed he'll be going till dark night, and he after eating nothing since the sun went up" (*Plays* 88). The Hiberno-English word "destroyed," meaning "wracked" or "exhausted," resonates prophetically with the standard English meaning of the word and foreshadows Bartley's death (Kiberd 81). Second, Synge borrowed the Irish literary and vernacular use of alliteration for *The Playboy of the Western World,* creating such phrases as "powers and potentates," "cot and cabin," and "fasting or fed" in which the alliteration enhances the synonymical or antonymical nature of the word pairs (Kiberd 107). Finally, he allowed the diction of the Irish vernacular to clash with Irish and English literary diction, producing startling juxtapositions. In the following quotation from *The Playboy,* Synge mixes Irish courtly love poetry, religious texts, and an earthy vernacular: "Amn't I after seeing the love-light of the star of knowledge shining from her brow, and hearing words would put you thinking on the holy Brigid speaking to the infant saints, and now she'll be turning again, and speaking hard words to me, like an old woman with a spavindy ass she'd have, urging on a hill" (*Plays* 51; Kiberd 162).

However, Synge's skill with words was not appreciated by many nationalists. Patrick Pearse, who believed that the national literature of Ireland could not possibly be written in English, was infuriated by the language of Synge's plays (Kiberd, *Synge* 5).[6] The critics argued that no peasant ever spoke as his did; Synge, who had not intended to reproduce peasant speech, nonetheless hit back by claiming that his work was almost entirely authentic dialogue. He wrote in the program note to *The Playboy* that "[n]early always when some friendly or angry critic tells me that such or such a phrase could not have been spoken by a peasant, he singles out some expression that I have heard, word for word, from some old woman or child" (qtd. in Greene and Stephens 254).

Synge's Hiberno-English was, like Lady Gregory's, much more a distillation than a literal rendering of peasant speech, which his insistence on authenticity belies. He did use words and phrases that he had heard in his travels, but he used them with an unusual frequency and density, creating a rich and beautiful language, but not a realistic one. Where Lady Gregory's Hiberno-English was spare and tight, Synge tended toward a more effusive style, creating vivid characters like Christy Mahon, the eponymous Playboy who could believably carry his language off.

Hyde, Lady Gregory, and Synge labored to create a form of English that would convey Irish themes, sentiments, syntax, and diction without betraying them into "buffoonery . . . [or] easy sentiment" (Gregory, *Theatre* 9), but their efforts were often criticized by other Irish people and sometimes by fellow renaissance writers. Like the dialect work of the Irish Renaissance, Harlem Renaissance dialect literature remains highly controversial to this day. From the artists' contemporaries like James Weldon Johnson to current critics such as Gayl Jones, reviewers, writers, and scholars have questioned dialect literature: Does it promote racial stereotypes? Can it be used successfully for serious literary endeavors? Even some writers like Paul Laurence Dunbar and Claude McKay who used dialect in their work did not feel that it was an uncompromised artistic form.

### Black America: My Hatred Tortures Me with Love

Within a few years of their arrival in America, slaves were usually proficient in standard English and an African-American dialect of English. Both languages were necessary, as some slave owners punished slaves for speaking standard English and some expected slaves, especially house servants, to speak it (Genovese 434, 439). The African-American dialects combined African and plantation vocabulary and grammar and added signifying, the use of word play to obscure meaning. White people complained about not being able to understand "nigger gibberish" and were frustrated by its ambiguities and double entendres: Eugene Genovese gives the example of a slave preacher praising runaway slaves to their owner, calling them "*ba-ad* niggers" (437). Irish speakers, who were known to greet landlords with "Soft morning, sor," would have appreciated the preacher's skill, as "sor" means "louse" in Irish (Kenner, *Colder Eye* 83).

After emancipation, however, African-American dialects were often considered shameful because of their association with minstrel shows and with Southern laborers, the lowest rung on the African-American social ladder. Although black and white speech patterns had influenced each other and converged to a degree, many intellectuals in both groups denigrated African-American dialects. Few black leaders were willing to acknowledge that dialect had been and could again be a source of cultural unity (Genovese 440, 438). Literary representation of dialect was considered limited at best, and likely to betray an author into stereotypical portrayals of African Americans. As James Weldon Johnson put it, dialect is "an instrument with but two full stops, humor and pathos" (*American Negro Poetry* xl).

Although Paul Laurence Dunbar died before the Harlem Renaissance truly began, his work foreshadows some of the interests of the younger generation of writers as well as some of the difficulties they would face. While fully two-thirds of Dunbar's poetry was written in standard English, his dialect poetry has attracted the majority of critical attention, and his intentions and racial politics are debated to this day.[7] Unlike Hyde and Lady Gregory, however, he was not an inspiration to the Harlem Renaissance writers who followed him.

Dunbar himself was ambivalent about his dialect poetry. He both held his dialect poems in high regard and regretted that publishers and interviewers did not seem to look beyond them to his standard English poetry. He felt that William Dean Howells's pronouncement favoring his dialect work had circumscribed his career (Howells, Introduction 630; Brawley, *Dunbar* 60), yet like Lady Gregory he stood up to those who criticized the idea of literature in dialect (Hudson 240). Although Dunbar's range may well have been limited by the demands of his audience, his dialect verse includes some interesting and controversial poetry.

Dunbar began writing at a time when regional American literature, which often used dialect to convey the characters' speech, was flourishing. The Indiana poet James Whitcomb Riley, one of Dunbar's models, wrote extremely popular poems such as "Little Orphan Annie" using the local Hoosier dialect. Regional writers were attempting to present their cultures to the mainstream, and dialects played a significant role in this endeavor. Another side to the use of dialect existed, however: for Southern regionalists like Thomas Nelson Page it enabled a sentimental rather than a critical perspective on the Old South. Such writers often used it to portray African Americans as contented, childlike creatures, justifying the pre- and postwar Southern approaches to race relations (MacKethan 211). In a somewhat similar vein, Dunbar's champion, William Dean Howells, felt that Dunbar's dialect poems "described the range between appetite and emotion . . . which is the range of the race" and "reveal[ed] . . . a finely ironical perception of the negro's limitations" (Introduction ix).

Dunbar's dialect poetry evokes both Riley and Page, as well as his own individual approach. Approximately one-sixth of his dialect poems are written in a white midwestern dialect, and several of his poems are heavily indebted to Riley for their themes (Simon 125). He even wrote a poem about Riley in which he praised the Hoosier poet's sentimental appeal. Dunbar has been accused of portraying African Americans in a negative manner in his black dialect verse,[8] but his white dialect poetry contains an equal number of unflattering portraits. For example, the African-American speaker in "Speakin' at de Cou't-House" shows no more ignorance than does the Hoosier speaker in "The Lawyer's Ways" who can't understand how the prosecuting and defense attorneys can paint such a different picture of the same defendant (Turner, "Dunbar" 71).

Although Dunbar did not attempt to justify slavery and peonage with his African-American vernacular work, as Page did, like Page's his poems sometimes present black speakers who are highly loyal to white people. For example, in "Chrismus on the Plantation," when the former master can no longer afford to pay the ex-slaves for their labor, "ol' Ben" says, "You kin jes' tell Mistah Lincum fu' to tek his freedom back," and all of the ex-slaves agree to work the plantation without pay.[9] The theme of loyalty reaches its apex in "The News." In this poem, an old blind slave decides to will his own death so that he can accompany his master, killed during the Civil War, to the afterlife. It concludes as follows:

Yes, suh, I's comin' ez fas' ez I kin,—
'Twas kin' o' da'k, but hit's lightah agin:
P'omised yo' pappy I'd allus tek keer
Of you,—yes, mastuh,—I's follerin'—hyeah! (137)

While some of Dunbar's poems appear to follow the conventions of what has been called the Plantation School of Southern regionalists, he also wrote several poems in which he expressed strong antislavery sentiments. In "An Ante-Bellum Sermon," a slave preacher cleverly disguises a message of freedom in his sermon about Moses. To throw informers off the track, he insists that he is merely "talkin' 'bout ouah freedom / In a Bibleistic way" (14), but he always comes back to the idea that "Moses wit his powah" will come and "set us chillun free" (15). Similarly, the speaker in "When Dey 'Listed Colored Soldiers" does not feel particularly conflicted when her lover 'Lias and their owner leave to fight on different sides in the Civil War. She feels little sympathy for the white women left behind except when she compares their situation to her own, and she is caught up in the excitement of watching African-American soldiers march off to battle. In the end, while "Mastah Jack" returns "broke for life" and "young mastah" lies dead in a ditch, 'Lias receives a hero's burial, covered in the American flag (183). The slave preacher and 'Lias's lover do not express the same deep loyalty to their owners as ol' Ben and the old blind slave do.

The majority of Dunbar's black dialect poems fall in between the Pagesque sentiments of "Chrismus on the Plantation" and "The News" and the antislavery poems like "An Ante-Bellum Sermon" and "When Dey 'Listed Colored Soldiers"; however, as Gayl Jones has said, his work "shared the consequences if not the intentions of the Plantation Tradition" (18). Although he did not intend them to do so, Dunbar's poems fed the racial assumptions of many white Americans and alienated many African Americans. Unlike many of the Irish Renaissance writers, however, his artistic goal was not to revise negative portrayals of his people but to explore the various linguistic means of representing them. He probably felt that some ideas were best expressed in dialect and others in standard English. In addition, his work may well have merely reflected attitudes toward slavery not uncommon among older African Americans.

As Eugene Genovese suggests, emancipated blacks often experienced "a compassion for others born of their own suffering . . . mutual obligations in an organic relationship, and a new sense of having the strength to reverse traditional roles within that organic relationship" (133).[10] The sentimental loyalty poems for which Dunbar is heavily criticized today may well be as accurate in their portrayals of African-American life as any of those that depict a desire for freedom or joy at the sight of black soldiers in uniform, and the two feelings need not be mutually exclusive.

Claude McKay was the first English-educated Jamaican of African descent to employ dialect as a primary poetic medium, and, like Dunbar, who broke similar ground in America, he was ambivalent about his work. As a young man, McKay was unsure about the merits of dialect poetry because his British-influenced education had depicted the Jamaican dialect as, in his words, "a vulgar tongue" ("Boyhood" 142). His mentor, an expatriate English folklore collector named Walter Jekyll, played William Dean Howells to his Dunbar and eventually convinced him to attempt more dialect verse.

With Jekyll's assistance, McKay published two collections of poetry in 1912, one in January entitled *Songs of Jamaica,* and one in November called *Constab Ballads.* The vast majority of the poems were in dialect, though a few were in standard English or had only occasional Jamaican words peppering the verse. McKay's books were favorably reviewed in Jamaica and elsewhere in the British empire, and the editor of the *Jamaica Times* called the publication of *Songs of Jamaica* "an event of note in Jamaican literature" (qtd. in Cooper, *Rebel* 50). During late 1911 and 1912, two Jamaican newspapers published additional dialect verse that had not gone into either of the books, often topical poems about social injustices (Cooper, *Rebel* 48, 54).

Although he was well-received by publishers and newspapers, McKay experienced a more negative reaction when he read from his work at various Jamaican literary clubs: the members repeatedly told him that although his poetry was "very nice and pretty," he was not "a real poet as Browning and Byron and Tennyson are poets" ("Boyhood" 142). Although these poets had been known to write in the vernacular themselves, to McKay and the club members they were the giants of nineteenth-century British literature. McKay's ambivalence about his dialect poetry was reinforced by these encounters, and his desire to return to standard English grew. As he wrote in "Boyhood in Jamaica," "I used to think I would show them something. Someday I would write poetry in straight English and amaze and confound them. They thought I was not serious, simply because I wrote poems in the dialect, which they did not consider becoming or profound" (142).

Dialect poetry proved troublesome for McKay in another way: he found it difficult to express in this form the intellectual questions that his education had raised. He read avidly about evolution, free will, and other contemporary philosophical topics. McKay's intellectual inquiries were as much a part of him as the local folk songs, but when he tried to express them in his poetry, the results were uneven. "Cudjoe Fresh from de Lecture" is a fair attempt at phrasing the theory of evolution in dialect. In this poem, Cudjoe rehashes for his cousin a lecture on evolution which he has just heard, emphasizing the aspects relevant to people of African descent:

> Me look 'pon me black 'kin, an' so me head grow big,
> Aldough me heaby han' dem hab fe plug an' dig;
> For ebery single man, no car' about dem rank,
> Him bring us ebery one an' put 'pon de same plank. (*Dialect* 55)

The lecturer had stated that all races of humanity were evolutionarily equal, and Cudjoe enthusiastically adopted this position as an alternative to the prevalent social Darwinism, which inevitably placed people of African descent in an inferior position.

But when McKay attempted in "To W. G. G." to express Schopenhauer's theory that an impersonal will controls human destinies, stating that we are but "[d]e helpless playt'ing of a Will," the blend of philosophical terms and dialect was less successful (*Dialect* 77). When he could create a character like Cudjoe who might plausibly be interested in certain issues and a context in which a speaker would be using dialect, McKay could successfully express his intellectual interests in dialect verse. That opportunity arose all too infrequently. Without plausible characters speaking the lines, his poems degenerate into philosophical preaching.

In August 1912, McKay left Jamaica for the United States, looking for suitable employment, a larger audience, and an answer to his qualms about dialect verse. He would never return to his homeland or to dialect poetry. Like Dunbar, McKay was ambivalent about his dialect verse, but, in a reversal of Dunbar's situation, in which a white audience wanted only dialect poetry, the Jamaican elite preferred standard English material. Because no demand existed for Jamaican dialect poetry in America either, upon moving there McKay was able to make the transition from dialect verse to standard English poetry. It is not clear why McKay gave up Jamaican dialect poetry: perhaps he felt that if it received mixed reviews in his homeland, it would be even less well regarded in another country. He certainly had no community of writers interested in dialect to support him and share his concerns, as Irish Renaissance writers did. Despite his difficulties with dialect poetry, however, McKay went on to write standard English poetry addressing racial issues and novels with characters who used a variety of black dialects.

Zora Neale Hurston was among the first African-American authors to publish dialect work without the ambivalence experienced by Dunbar and McKay. In 1925, Hurston, author of several short stories and a play, used her contacts in New York City to acquire a scholarship at Barnard. She became the student of Franz Boas, perhaps the leading American anthropologist of his time. Boas stressed scientific objectivism and precise fieldwork, and under his tutelage Hurston learned to see her own native culture—the all-black town of Eatonville, Florida—through "the spyglass of Anthropology" (*Mules* 1). By 1927 she felt ready to go into the field, but the culture of Eatonville and that of Barnard were not so easily amalgamated: Hurston spent six frustrating months trying to collect folklore in Florida, wavering between what she termed "carefully accented Barnardese" and her native dialect (*Dust* 175). Boas had taught her the most advanced techniques of the time, but Hurston would need to develop her own style of collecting, one based less on objectivity than on cultural immersion, which actually anticipated later anthropological practices.

Hurston soon found the funding to spend the next two years collecting folklore, this time much more successfully, and as she worked, she thought about ways of bringing the material to the public. She believed that presenting the intricate verbal play of rural African Americans to white and urban African-American audiences would demonstrate that material poverty did not entail a similar cultural state. To this end, Hurston corresponded with Langston Hughes regarding the possibility of collaborating on an opera or play about the life of the folk. In the spring of 1930, they settled in New Jersey and began to write *Mule Bone*.

Hurston and Hughes believed they could replace the stereotypes found in minstrel shows and on Broadway with more accurate, yet equally entertaining, portrayals of African-American life. *Mule Bone* is packed with the oral culture of the rural African-American south: the characters tell tales and attempt to outdo one another in stories and in courtship; they sing in church, while dancing, and in children's games; above all, they articulate the verbal rituals of Hurston's childhood. Every aspect of life represented contains rich verbal moments: when the men contemplate beating their wives, they use four different expressions, including "I'd stomp her till she rope like okra" (52); when Sister Jones leaves the stage, she says, "see y'all later an tell you straighter" (102). Like Synge and Lady Gregory, Hurston condensed the speech she had heard and the activities she had seen, creating a vivid style, if not entirely a realistic one.

Before the revisions of the manuscript were completed, Hurston and Hughes quarreled about the rights to their play. The bitter dispute over *Mule Bone* ended their friendship, and the play was never finished. In 1991, it was staged for the first time at the Lincoln Center Theatre in New York, but in a bowdlerized form, for the producers had found that Hurston and Hughes were not entirely successful in revising dramatic portrayals of African Americans, and they decided to make revisions of their own, cutting material that they considered racist and sexist, such as the references to spousal abuse (Bass 2–3).

The *Mule Bone* fiasco had not soured Hurston on the theater, however, and, as she was having trouble publishing *Mules and Men,* her book of folklore, she turned to the stage as an outlet for her ideas. Hurston began her professional theater work in New York, where she helped write *Fast and Furious* and *Jungle Scandals.* As the titles suggest, these revues presented stereotypes of African-American culture, a far cry from Hurston's goals for the theater. Fortunately, both faded quickly, and Hurston decided to create her own theatrical piece, a depiction of one day in the life of a railroad work camp entitled *The Great Day.* Like *Mule Bone, The Great Day* is replete with elements of rural southern African-American oral culture: work songs, sermons, games, conjuring, and the blues. Even with a last-minute loan, Hurston could only afford to stage the show for one night in January 1932, but a large crowd turned out and reviews were positive. During the next few years, Hurston organized several more performances of the material in *The Great Day* as part of her ongoing attempt to bring a more authentic depiction of African-American folk cultures to American audiences. One production, *From Sun to Sun,* toured central Florida in 1933 with a cast composed largely of friends and family from Eatonville.[11] The program featured songs, such as "John Henry" and "Let the Deal Go Down," and a variety of dances, including a Bahaman fire dance and the Crow Dance, and a one-act play by Hurston that was based on a folktale (O'Sullivan and Lane 138–39).

In most of her novels, Hurston attempted to infuse folklore and dialect into a prose art form much as she had done in her theatrical work. Some African-American reviewers were troubled by her novels because they felt that she had focussed on folkways at the expense of other aspects of her craft, including the appropriate political approach. Richard Wright wrote in *New Masses* that *Their Eyes Were Watching God* catered to a racist white audience: "Miss Hurston *voluntarily* continues in her novel the tradition which was *forced* upon the Negro in the theater, that is, the minstrel technique which makes the "white folks" laugh. Her characters eat and laugh and cry and work and kill; they swing like a pendulum eternally in that safe and narrow orbit in which America likes to see the Negro live: between laughter and tears" (25).

Wright labeled Hurston's prose "facile sensuality" and said her novel lacked theme and social message. Similarly, Alain Locke wrote in an *Opportunity* review that Hurston's emphasis in *Their Eyes Were Watching God* on "poetic phras[ing]" and "rare dialect and folk humor" restrained her work on a surface level and prevented her from "diving down deep either to the inner psychology of characterization or to sharp analysis of the social background" ("Jingo" 10). Neither critique is particularly accurate, perhaps because of the stylistic and political preferences of the reviewers. Both reveal their bias toward what Locke terms "social document fiction": as two of many African-American intellectuals who turned toward communism in the 1930s, Locke and Wright emphasized socialist realism over Hurston's "folklore fiction." They may have also been unable to perceive a black woman's struggle with sexism and racism as sufficiently political: as the Invisible Man would later puzzle, "why did they [women] insist upon confusing the class struggle with the ass struggle . . . ?" (Ellison 418).

Like Synge, despite the negative reviews of her novels by several politically motivated critics, Hurston was the most successful of the writers in her movement at integrating an African-American vernacular into literature. Perhaps this was because she was using her native dialect and did not attempt to work in poetry, whose status as the highest of literary forms caused anxiety in other writers, such as McKay. Dunbar often separated his dialect and standard English verse and felt that he had been railroaded into writing mainly dialect poetry, and McKay abandoned dialect verse for standard English poetry when he moved to America; Hurston used dialect in conjunction with standard English throughout her career to represent rural African-American life.

Like Irish writers battling England's "cultural invasion," African-American dialect writers faced an arduous struggle. Many black people rejected their work as low and inartistic, and though white Americans frequently praised it, this praise was often marked by condescension. Harlem and Irish Renaissance writers addressed similar language issues, but while the Irish dialect writers often read each other's works, commented on them, and were inspired by them to further the technique, the Harlem Renaissance writers did not work together so closely on dialect literature: Dunbar died young before the movement really began; McKay had only Walter Jekyll to encourage him in Jamaica; and Hurston approached African-American dialects largely from the anthropologist's perspective, using as resources the people of the South rather than her literary peers. When Hurston and Langston Hughes did attempt to work together on *Mule Bone,* it was not the collaboration of two *rural* dialect writers—Hurston was the acknowledged expert—and their quarrel was facilitated by this uneven partnership. The story of dialect literature in the Harlem Renaissance is one of great adversity, both intentional and unintentional, from within African-American communities and from without. Perhaps it was so because the writers lacked the intellectual interaction on language issues enjoyed by their counterparts in the Irish Renaissance, which itself may have been caused by the low status of African-American dialects of English.

# 3

# The Entanglement of Origins
## Questions of Identity

The Negro is not. Any more than the white man.
*Franz Fanon*

[T]he Irish race is at present in a most anomalous position,
imitating England and yet apparently hating it.
*Douglas Hyde*

In the introduction to *The Invention of Ethnicity,* Werner Sollors writes that "[e]thnic groups are typically imagined as if they were natural, real, eternal, stable, and static units. They seem to be always already in existence" (xii-xiv). As Sollors argues and the experiences of African Americans and Irish people indicate, race and ethnicity possess none of these qualities.[1] The very terms "African American," "black," and "Irish" are complex constructions which belie the liminality of race and ethnicity. The president of the NAACP from 1931 to 1955, Walter White, was white in appearance and largely Caucasian genetically yet identified culturally as black. Many members of the Irish Renaissance were of English descent, but they asserted that they were Irish writers.

To the same degree that these categories are social constructions, they are also powerful social facts: Houston Baker's "taxi fallacy" reminds us that though race (and gender) is a social construction, black men often have difficulty finding a cab (186).[2] This tension between construction and fact creates great difficulties for those who attempt to define a racial or ethnic identity. As Diana Fuss phrases it, "to advocate [a] . . . rigid essentialist view which holds that 'race' is self-evidently hereditary or biologistic can . . . interfere with an analysis of the ideological and political formation of racial subjects"; on the other hand, "to maintain a strict constructionist view which holds that there is no such thing [as] racial identity can block our understanding of the social production of 'race'" (92).

### Constructing Ethnicity and Race

Essentialist definitions of Irishness and blackness have until recently dominated social science and persist in popular culture to this day. While Americans have long possessed a unitary view of race that greatly distorts the realities of racial mixing, English and Catholic Irish people have often perceived difference where it does not necessarily exist. By the late nineteenth century, English people had long felt uncomfortable with Ireland, their only colony with white natives, and they frequently tried to construct Irish people as racially different. When they could not, they were distressed. After visiting rural Ireland in 1860, Charles Kingsley wrote, "I am haunted by the human chimpanzees I saw . . . to see white chimpanzees is dreadful; if they were black, one would not feel it so much, but their skins, except where tanned by exposure, are as white as ours" (308). In the second half of the nineteenth century, English scientists began to assert that what they called Celts and Saxons were not pure racial groups, as they had been mixing for many years. Their findings were not quickly adopted by the mainstream: at that time English popular culture was caught up in a cult of Saxon purity that required Irish people to be racially distinct (Gilley 91, 94).

Rather than attacking racial construction, many Irish people posited their own Irish essence. In response to theories like Beddoe's Index of Nigrescence, Dr. Richard Tuthill Massy used the pseudoscience of physiognomy to prove that Celts were actually superior to Anglo-Saxons (L. Curtis 16). Journalist D. P. Moran and many of his fellow nationalists polarized Catholic Irish and Anglo-Irish culture, denying their history of interaction and intermarriage. Moran was so virulently opposed to cultural interaction that he called Irish literature in English "a mongrel thing" and refused to accept it as part of Irish culture (qtd. in Lyons 60). However, it would have been more accurate for Irish nationalists to proclaim as one of their Italian counterparts did after the unification of Italy in 1860, "We have made Italy; now we must make Italians" (qtd. in Stein 83).

Another difference between the ordering of racial and ethnic groups in Ireland and in America was the belief of some Victorian English intellectuals, including Matthew Arnold and Charles Kingsley, that the mixing of Celtic and Saxon stock would prove beneficial to the English (Gilley 86). Many English people believed that "Celts" could be socially rehabilitated, if they would only make an effort to conform to English norms (Gilley 93). On the other hand, most white Americans dreaded miscegenation and legislated against it, and most African Americans did not approve of it any more than white people did. In America, racial mixing was frequently believed to produce physical and moral degeneracy: light-skinned blacks without impeccable family reputations were considered morally suspect by both blacks and whites (Davis 25, 57).

Race has been defined and determined differently at various times in American history, but, as Judith Stein states, "[t]he defining of people of African descent has always been, and remains, associated with the contemporary political purposes" (103). To this assertion one ought to add that both whites and blacks have participated in the definition-making. Americans, both black and white, have usually defined a black person as one with any known sub-Saharan African ancestry. Some people with very few black ancestors have tried to challenge the definition in court, but as recently as 1986 the Supreme Court allowed this "one-drop rule" to stand when it refused to hear a case brought by a woman who wished her passport to read "white." Her black ancestry included approximately three of thirty-two great-great-great grandparents. Black communities tend to react similarly: when Walter White married a white woman, many black people were outraged because he had married outside the community with which he had affiliated himself (Davis 5, 10–11, 7).[3] As Mary Waters writes, "[b]lack Americans . . . are highly socially constrained to identify as blacks, without other options available to them, even when they believe or know that their forebears included many non-blacks" (18).

Federal and state apparatus such as the census and birth certificates have supported arbitrary definitions of race like the one-drop rule. Between 1840 and 1910, the U.S. Bureau of the Census counted whites, mulattos, and blacks—and the enumerators were not always given definitions of these terms. Beginning in 1920, all people with any black ancestors were counted as black. When self-identification began in 1960, no large fluctuation in racial populations occurred, indicating that most black people accepted the one-drop rule (Davis 11–12).

Neither African Americans nor Irish people are particularly pure groups, but for many years both the dominant and the subaltern cultures, particularly in America, found benefits in constructing them as such. In the end, the results of racial and ethnic polarization in both Ireland and America were inaccurate constructions of identity, distrust of those who did not fit the templates, and ostracism of those who attempted to cross the lines.

## Constructions of Irishness

As Ireland recovered from the Famine in the second half of the nineteenth century, the country was economically dependent on England and the Irish language was quickly disappearing. To some, it seemed the last opportunity for cultural renewal and autonomy: could Ireland reestablish a national identity or would English culture dominate? And if Irish culture could be salvaged, what shape would this national identity take? As in black America, the identity being discussed was a construction more than reality.

Three of the elements important to those who wished to construct an Irish identity were the past, the peasants, and religion. The ancient Irish past appealed to many because it predated sectarianism, stood out from the mythology of other countries, and seemed more appealing than the often-sordid present (Marcus 224). Yeats believed that without infusions of ancient history, literature would be vitiated. As he wrote in "The Celtic Element in Literature," "literature dwindles to a mere chronicle of circumstance, or passionless fantasies, and passionless meditations, unless it is constantly flooded with the passions and beliefs of ancient times" (*Essays* 185). Yeats and many of his contemporaries believed that the past was "the subject for and source of creativity" (Sanders 5), but others wondered what use it could be to a modern, progressive society.

Another problem lay in the fragmented nature of Irish history. Seamus Deane writes that "[t]he principle of continuity which he [Yeats] established in literature stretching from Swift to the Revival [the Irish Renaissance] and that which [Patrick] Pearse established in politics stretching from Wolfe Tone [who led a revolt in 1798] to the men of 1916 are both exemplary instances of the manner in which tradition becomes an instrument for the present. Without such a tradition, or the idea of it, history appears gapped, discontinuous, unmanageably complex" (36). Yeats and Pearse, people with quite different plans for Ireland, both recognized the need for a unitary Irish history.

Yeats attempted to create a space for the Anglo-Irish by constructing an Anglo-Irish intellectual and political tradition dating to the eighteenth century. In the title poem of his book *The Tower* (1928), Yeats imagines he is writing his will, and he nominates as his heirs "[t]he people of Burke and of Grattan," eighteenth century Anglo-Irish political figures who, he asserts, were "[b]ound neither to Cause nor to State" (*Poems* 198). Similarly, Pearse offered an unbroken chain of revolutionaries to which a present-day nationalist might connect. During his 1915 speech at the funeral of Irish Republican Brotherhood (IRB) leader Jeremiah O'Donovan Rossa, Pearse urged the use of physical force to gain independence, saying, "we know only one definition of freedom: it is [Wolfe] Tone's definition, it is [John] Mitchel's definition, it is Rossa's definition" (134–35). Because Ireland's history, unlike England's, was not perceived as an orderly progress, a unitary construct of Irish history was highly useful to theorists of Irishness with a variety of goals (Gibbons 103, 105).[4]

Irish peasants were also useful to nationalist and literary constructions of Irishness. Needing a way to rebut the evident material advantages of England, many nationalists deemed the penurious western peasants the best of the Irish, pure and pious people free of English-bred materialism. John Synge's most controversial play, *The Playboy of the Western World*, represented the peasants so differently from this nationalist ideal that one disgusted spectator wrote in his diary, "*The Playboy* is not a truthful or just picture of the Irish peasants, but simply the outpouring of a morbid, unhealthy mind ever seeking on the dunghill of life for the nastiness that lies concealed there" (Holloway 181).

The peasants were also useful to several of the Irish Renaissance writers who, like many of the political nationalists, rejected what they perceived as the effect of English materialism on literature. Ironically, Synge, who so outraged narrow-minded nationalist sensibilities, was among these writers. As he wrote in the preface to *The Playboy*, "in countries where the imagination of the people, and the language they use, is rich and living, it is possible for a writer to be rich and copious with his words. . . . In the modern literature of towns, however, richness is found only in sonnets, or prose poems, or in one or two elaborate books that are far away from the profound and common interests of life" (3–4). Synge believed that industrial culture was ruining literature and that the best work was being done in countries like Ireland with a strong peasant base.

One of the most important elements of the nationalist elevation of the peasantry was their alleged piety, and religion played an important role in the nationalist construction of Irish identity. As R. F. Foster writes, "Catholicism in the post-Famine age provided a highly organized, coherent identity that helped Irish society cope with the psychological impact of disruption" (340). As the nineteenth century drew to a close, Catholicism played an increasingly active role in Irish life as temperance and devotional societies flourished. Although the Catholic Church usually opposed Irish nationalism in the nineteenth and early twentieth centuries, nationalist and Catholic attitudes converged as Pearse and his ascetic young companions took over the main cultural and political organizations. Pearse once described Irish revolutionary Robert Emmet, executed in 1803, as "dying that his people might live, even as Christ died" (71).[5]

Meanwhile, some Irish Renaissance members showed an interest in another sort of religion, spiritualism, which they linked to the peasants through their fairy lore. Many of the writers collected stories from the country people and asserted that the old beliefs still lived. The young Yeats went a step further and suggested that some city audiences believed the stories as well. In 1889 he wrote that in two lectures on "Irish goblins" by Theosophical Society cofounder Henry Steel Olcott, "[h]e asserted that such things really exist, and so strangely has our modern world swung back on its old belief, so far has the reaction from modern materialism gone, that his audience seemed rather to agree with him" (*New Island* 17).

These three elements, the past, the peasants, and religion, are all means to reject English culture: by emphasizing them, Irish nationalists and writers could distance themselves from what they perceived as the ugly, urban, material life of England. Unfortunately, this approach created a more negative than a positive collective identity: Irishness was being defined as "not-Englishness" (Boyce 249). Like African Americans adopting the racial polarizations of mainstream white culture, constructors of Irishness had difficulty seeing beyond the dichotomy.

Occasionally, however, a writer or political figure would condemn the notion of racial essences. Thomas MacDonagh, an Irish nationalist and writer, decried the concept that racial essences influenced literary accomplishments: "I have little sympathy with the criticism that marks off subtle qualities in literature as altogether racial, that refuses to admit

natural exceptions in such a naturally exceptional thing as high literature, attributing only the central body to the national genius, the marginal portions to this alien strain or that" (57). MacDonagh's attitude
was, however, uncommon.

### Constructions of Blackness

Harlem Renaissance writers addressed several of the putative elements of
a black identity in their work, including the belief that African Americans
were a more emotional race than Caucasians and the notion that blacks
possessed an artistic gift. They also pondered the question of the past,
specifically, the role of an African heritage in twentieth-century black
life. Since the Enlightenment, several European philosophers, including
David Hume and G. W. F. Hegel, had asserted that a dichotomy existed
between Africans and Caucasians. The former were considered an inferior, more emotional race, and the latter, a superior, more intellectual
race. Like Irish approaches to Irishness, black theories of race in the early
twentieth century often accepted this polarization but reversed the terms,
so that the emotional was privileged over the cerebral. In his novel *Home
to Harlem,* Claude McKay presented several cabaret scenes that depict
African Americans as highly sensual and emotional: "[h]ere are none of
the well-patterned, well-made emotions of the respectable world. A laugh
might finish in a sob. A moan end in hilarity. That gorilla type wriggling
there with his hands so strangely hugging his mate, may strangle her
tonight. But he has no thought of that now. He loves the warm wriggle
and is lost in it. Simple, raw emotions and real" (178). Similarly, in her
essay "How It Feels to Be Colored Me," Zora Neale Hurston describes
visiting a jazz club with a white friend: "I dance wildly inside myself; I
yell within, I whoop; I shake my assegai above my head, I hurl it true to
the mark *yeeeeooww!* . . . I creep back slowly to the veneer we call
civilization with the last tone and find the white friend sitting motionless
in his seat, smoking calmly" (154).

For many Harlem Renaissance writers, the notion of a racial essence
played a key part in racial pride: in both of these passages, black culture
appears vivid and emotional, and Hurston also contrasts it to white
culture. Although such beliefs can provide ammunition for racial prejudice, many prominent African Americans clung to them during the 1920s
(Hemenway 76). Some were ambivalent: in July of 1926, W. E. B. Du
Bois wrote that "it is probably true that tropical and sub-tropical peoples
have more vivid imagination, are accustomed to expressing themselves

with greater physical and spiritual abandon than most folk" ("Krigwa" 134). But in October of the same year, he suggested that the reason DuBose Heyward did not set *Porgy and Bess* in a white community was not because white people express themselves with less "physical and spiritual abandon" than black people, but because "they would drum him out of town. The only chance he had to tell the truth of pitiful human degradation was to tell it of colored people" ("Criteria" 297). Du Bois and a few other African Americans sometimes perceived race as an essence and sometimes as a construction, but most people simply accepted the former.

The emphasis on racial essence played itself out in the ideas of African-American intellectuals on the relation of race to art. Many believed that the purported black emotional qualities were highly suitable for the arts and that drama would be their special venue. As playwright Randolph Edmonds put it, "[t]here is drama in Negro life . . . suffering, struggle, comedy, atmosphere, and great emotional crises—the very essence of the dramatic—are found abundantly in Negro life" (303). Dramatist Willis Richardson agreed with Edmonds and even claimed that "the mellowness of his [the African-American's] voice" was part of the race's "natural ability for fine acting" (338). Not only dramatists believed that African Americans had a special gift to bring to the stage. In her essay "The Gift of Laughter" in *The New Negro*, novelist Jessie Fauset wrote that "[a]ll about him [the black person] and within himself stalks the conviction that like the Irish, the Russian, and the Magyar he has some peculiar offering which shall contain the very essence of the drama" (161).

As Nathan Huggins suggests, many African Americans claimed an artistic essence in their race because they felt that "[a]bandoning all distinction was a total rejection of the past, a kind of self-obliteration. Those qualities of American life which had germinated in black soil had to be explained. The spiritual, the music, the dance, the language were distinct because they were from a Negro source. Without distinct Negro character, there could be no Negro genius" (*Harlem* 151). By positing an artistic racial essence, African-American intellectuals could suggest that black people, like various peoples of European descent, had an important contribution to make to world culture. Since drama was a popular art form across America and Europe in the early twentieth century and black people were believed to have qualities that would suit the theater well, a number of African Americans felt they ought to attempt it.

Because, like the Irish, they believed possessing a noble past facilitates gaining respect in the present, African Americans theorizing racial identity had to address their African heritage. As Arthur Schomberg, a patron of the Harlem Renaissance, wrote, "[t]he American Negro must remake his past in order to make his future" (217). Mainstream American culture perceived Africa as "the dark continent," an uncivilized and unknowable place, and many African Americans accepted this portrayal. In his novel *Nigger Heaven*, Carl Van Vechten depicts a well-to-do black family that completely rejects an African heritage. When another character tries to interest them in an African sculpture exhibit, the daughter, Hester, says emphatically, "It's the work of heathen savages . . . and it has nothing to do with art" (70).

Sentiments like Hester's were common, as were ambivalent feelings about Africa. Countee Cullen's poem "Heritage" explores these mixed emotions. The speaker begins with the assertion that the "[g]reat drums" of Africa pound in his ears and the "dark blood dammed within" him is about to burst out.[6] His African heritage seems to be very strong, even dangerously so, although he expresses it mainly through exotic clichés of jungles and drums. As the poem progresses, the speaker seems to reject an African heritage, asking, "What is last year's snow to me, / Last year's anything?" (52–53). He disclaims any emotional connection to or value in the African past: even the literary allusion in this line is to the medieval French poet François Villon, not to an African source. The feelings he has denied return, however, and the speaker admits that "in my heart / Do I play a double part" (97–98). He feels that he must either deny or be overwhelmed by Africa, and he does not find a more comfortable intermediate position in the poem. Other black people who more successfully reclaimed Africa for themselves often went no deeper than the images Cullen's speaker associated with Africa, images which fit the paradigm of the sensual, emotional African American. Despite the difficulties presented by the negative image of Africa, as in Ireland, "[i]t was assumed that if Afro-Americans were to have an art and literature of distinctiveness and character, and if blacks were to achieve the self-respect that would be essential to winning equality in America, they would have to reconstruct and use their history and folk tradition" (Huggins, *Voices* 216).

Not all African Americans of the 1920s accepted the notion of a racial essence: in his 1926 essay in the *Nation,* "The Negro-Art Hokum," satirist George Schuyler documented the similarities between white and black life and concluded that "it is sheer nonsense to talk about 'racial differences' as between the American black man and the American white man" (663). Schuyler also pointed out that the belief in racial essences was supported by racist pseudo-scientists and "the patriots who flood the treasury of the Ku Klux Klan," and he urged his readers to reject it "with a loud guffaw" (663). Most of them, including many prominent African-American intellectuals and writers, did not. Schuyler could not place his article for a year, and when the *Nation* finally printed it, the editors solicited a counter-argument from Langston Hughes for the next issue. Despite the work of people like Schuyler, polarized theories of race would continue to be popular with both blacks and whites for many years. As Leslie Catherine Sanders phrases it, "[d]uring the 1920s . . . by exploiting racial characteristics when creating Negro characters, both black and white writers deliberately opposed black and white in the American imaginative world" (7). Like Thomas MacDonagh, Schuyler rejected the idea that racial essences played a role in literature, but neither man's voice was heard by the majority in Ireland and America.

### Questioning Commitment: The Anglo-Irish Dilemma

Defining one's cultural identity in Ireland at the turn of the century was not an easy task, and it was even more difficult for the Anglo-Irish, caught between their emotional connections to England and to Ireland. Many Anglo-Irish people looking for an anchor for their loyalty turned to the Gaelic League or other forms of Irish political and cultural activity, but their interest in their country was not enough for many Catholic nationalists who were, as Joseph O'Brien phrases it, "deeply suspicious of and almost congenitally insensitive to" Anglo-Irish nationalist feelings (51). Many, like journalist D. P. Moran, could not accept Anglo-Irish support because they perceived Ireland as the battleground of two anti-thetical cultures, one Gaelic Catholic and the other Anglo-Irish (Lyons 61). Others, like author and critic Daniel Corkery, were somewhat more accommodating; however, Corkery described the coming to nationalism of an Anglo-Irish person as a "conversion" and a "rebirth," not an easy or natural process, and he defined the three forces in "the Irish national being" as religion, nationalism, and the land, all of which he found to be tremendous stumbling stones for Anglo-Irish writers (54, 19). Only Synge's work satisfied him, and that in one play alone, *Riders to the Sea,* a lyrical tragedy.

Despite the hectoring of the extremists and the suspicion of the moderates, a number of Anglo-Irish people worked to create a cultural fusion and bring the two sides closer together. As Yeats wrote, they hoped to "[p]reserve that which is living and help the two Irelands, Gaelic Ireland and Anglo-Ireland, so to unite that neither shall shed its pride" (*Explorations* 337). But there was much of which the Anglo-Irish could not be proud, such as the isolation and profligacy that caused three of Lady Gregory's brothers to facilitate their deaths with alcohol and prompted historian Standish James O'Grady to describe the Ascendancy as "rotting from the land" (Kohfeldt 125; O'Grady 180). Cultural fusion required a more vital and hardy Anglo-Irish population than existed at the beginning of the twentieth century. In the series of poems entitled "Meditations in Time of Civil War," Yeats celebrated the great country houses and the vital people who had inhabited them, but he acknowledged their decay and the uncertainty of their survival: "And maybe the great-grandson of that house, / For all its bronze and marble, 's but a mouse" (*Poems* 200). In the years since the Irish Renaissance, the dream of an Anglo-Irish identity has practically disappeared: about a tenth of the great houses were destroyed during the war for Irish independence and the civil war in the early 1920s, and since then many have collapsed or have been sold for their bricks, with the Protestant population of the Republic of Ireland steadily diminishing.

Because of their troubled and complex history in relation to Ireland, Anglo-Irish people faced an extra dimension of difficulty in the search for cultural identity. As Hugh Kenner states of the Anglo-Irish Renaissance members, "[t]heir node of loyalty should have been John Bull. But, Romantics all, they cherished the Romantic dream, Shelley's dream, liberty: in their land, as it proved, an Irish Bull, not John. Yet none of them could disengage from the entanglements of origins" (*Colder Eye* 269). It is common to attack the Irish Renaissance for its overwhelmingly middle- and upper-class Anglo-Irish composition, but it could not easily have been otherwise.[7] As Tom Nairn asserts, revolutions are quite often led by the children of the bourgeoisie: "[i]n its most typical version, this assumed the shape of a restless middle-class and intellectual leadership trying to stir up and channel popular class energies into support for the new states" (41).[8] Few Catholic Irish people had the time, interest, and distaste for propaganda to commit to a literary movement of this nature. For many Anglo-Irish people, the study of Ireland's language, lore, and literature surpassed dilettantism—it provided access to a cultural identity that they sorely desired. Although no real equivalent to the Anglo-Irish exists in American race relations, Harlem Renaissance artists have also been criticized for their largely middle-class, urban origins, and white participants were treated with suspicion by some black and white people.[9] In addition, if an Irish identity was too narrowly defined, excluding people who truly wanted to be Irish, including many of the Anglo-Irish, an African-American identity was often too broadly defined, including people who did not necessarily self-identify as black, like Jean Toomer.

## Questioning Commitment: Poet or Negro Poet

Constructions of racial or ethnic identity inevitably render marginal people who do not accept them. During the Harlem Renaissance, some writers were criticized because they rejected the label "Negro poet" or "Negro writer." Because racial identification was encouraged by both black and white intellectuals, these writers were treated with suspicion and their desire not to be labeled went unheeded. The problem first arose shortly before the Harlem Renaissance. In his biography of Paul Laurence Dunbar, Benjamin Brawley wrote that "[h]e felt that he was first of all a man, then an American, and incidentally a Negro" (77). In an 1898 interview, Dunbar indicated that this conception of life extended to poetry: "[black] poetry will not be exotic or differ much from that of the whites. . . . For two hundred and fifty years the environment of the Negro has been American, in every respect the same as that of all other Americans" (qtd. in Brawley, *Dunbar* 77). But Dunbar's audience was not responding to him as an American poet. Reader and publishers largely preferred his dialect verse; as he phrased it in "The Poet," "the world, it turned to praise / A jingle in a broken tongue" (191). A number of his poems lament the African-American condition at the turn of the century, such as "Sympathy," which states, "I know why the caged bird sings" (102); "We Wear the Mask" can also be read as a lament for the strictures Dunbar faced as a writer. Unfortunately, this issue did not pass with Dunbar, and it went on to plague the next generation of African-American writers as well.

Countee Cullen and Jean Toomer followed Dunbar in aspiring to be thought of as poets rather than as African-American poets. Like Dunbar, Countee Cullen became popular with the American mainstream at an early age, a rare experience then for an African-American writer. His first book of poems, *Colors*, was published in 1925 when he was twenty-two, and he commanded enough respect to be able to publish an anthology of poetry by African-American writers only two years later. Cullen's convictions about race and poetry developed early: in 1924 he told a reporter, "[i]f I am going to be a poet at all, I am going to be POET and not NEGRO POET" (*Song* 23). He associated the term "Negro poet" with the emphasis on racial propaganda within African-American communities, and he felt that attempts to produce propaganda poetry had hampered African-American writers. Cullen did not avoid racial subject matter—one of his most famous poems describes being called a nigger at age eight—or deny his racial identity—he married the daughter of W. E. B. Du Bois; he merely resented the push toward racial propaganda.

Cullen used the introduction to his anthology, *Caroling Dusk,* to further explain his position on race and poetry. He stated that he had entitled the collection "an anthology of verse by Negro poets" and not "an anthology of Negro verse" because he did not believe African-American writers were as distinct from other American writers as, for example, Chinese ones were. In contrast to Dunbar, Cullen did not deny that African-American poetry might have certain distinguishing characteristics, but he did feel that it generally resembled mainstream American poetry and owed a great deal more to "the rich background of English and American poetry" than to "an African inheritance" (xi).

Although many of Cullen's poems treat racial subjects, he strongly advocated that African-American writers should have the freedom to explore the subject matter of their choice, whether it be racial or nonracial. He often used his column in the Urban League's journal *Opportunity* to inveigh against limiting the range of African-American writers. For example, he criticized one Frank L. Mott for implying that black writers should address racial subjects, writing, "at his dictum that an author *ought,* by virtue of birth or any other circumstance, be interested solely in any *particular* thing . . . we utter protest" ("Tower" 180). Cullen took a clear stand on the issues surrounding race and poetry: he rejected the label of "Negro poet" not because he denied his heritage, but because he felt it pushed African-American writers toward propaganda, distorted their influences, and limited the topics available to them.

Like Cullen, Jean Toomer did not like to be called a "Negro writer," but in his case it was not because he had artistic objections to the term, but because he did not always identify himself as an African American. Toomer's heritage was complex: his maternal grandparents and his paternal grandmother were all of mixed race and his paternal grandfather was white. Young Jean spent his childhood in a white milieu, had a white stepfather, and did not live in an African-American community until he was fifteen. Like many members of his family, he could live as a white person if he chose to do so. He made friends in both the Harlem and Greenwich Village writers' circles, where he often argued that he did not want to be labeled a "Negro writer" because he believed that the various races would eventually become one in a sort of racial fusion. As he wrote in 1930, "[t]here is a new race in America. I am a member of this new race. It is neither black nor white nor in between. It is the American race . . . the old divisions into white, black, brown, red are outworn in this country" (qtd. in Byrd 314).

Toomer is best known, however, for *Cane,* a lyrical depiction of African-American life, especially the rural black South. *Cane* was written after he had lived in Sparta, Georgia, for a few months in 1921—his first venture into the Deep South. Several of the characters are of mixed race themselves, including Esther, who has a "chalk-white" complexion (20); Fernie May Rosen, whose nose was "aquiline, Semitic" (14); and Becky's biracial sons, described as follows: "White or colored? No one knew, and least of all themselves. . . . 'Godam the white folks; godam the niggers,' they shouted as they left town" (6). Toomer surely sympathized with their predicament: the foreword to *Cane* referred to him as a Negro, limiting his racial identity to one of its several facets.

Because most people perceived race as highly polarized and, as Langston Hughes put it, "the Negro was in vogue" (*Sea* 228), Toomer was not able to shed the label "Negro writer" (Byrd 315–16). The prominent black intellectual William Stanley Braithwaite referred to him as "a bright morning star of a new day of the race in literature" (qtd. in Turner, Introduction ix). His publisher spoke of him as a "colored genius" and emphasized his African-American heritage in advertising copy (Kerman and Eldridge 110). Well-known white writers such as Sherwood Anderson told him not to let white aesthetics "spoil" him (Lewis 59). Toomer's rejection of the "Negro writer" label intensified as the pressure to identify himself as African American and to write on racial subjects grew. He complained that Alain Locke had included his work in *The New Negro* against his wishes (Byrd 316). He admonished his publisher for playing up one aspect of his heritage, writing, "I must insist that you never use such a word, such a thought again" (Lewis 71). And, concerning Anderson, he bemoaned to a friend, "Sherwood limits me to Negro" (Kerman and Eldridge 97). At first, Toomer was willing to acknowledge African-American ancestry as part of his racial makeup, but the emphasis on racial dichotomy frustrated him and caused him to take increasingly radical stances: in at least one of his autobiographical fragments, he claimed to have no "Negro blood" (qtd. in Lewis 61).

Langston Hughes's 1926 essay "The Negro Artist and the Racial Mountain" is directly addressed to writers like Cullen and Toomer who rejected the label of "Negro writer." As Hughes relates it, "[o]ne of the most promising of the young Negro poets said to me once, 'I want to be a poet—not a Negro poet,' meaning, I believe, 'I want to write like a white poet'; meaning subconsciously, 'I would like to be a white poet'; meaning behind that, 'I would like to be white'" (692). Hughes felt that such people were filled with self-hatred, but while this feeling troubled many African Americans, Cullen and Toomer were not necessarily among them. Both men had other explanations for not wishing to be called "Negro writers," and Cullen never rejected his African-American ancestry, but Hughes connected the desire not to be a Negro poet to the drive for assimilation prevalent among African Americans, and he believed it would cripple their artistic powers. Hughes did assert in this essay that artists ought to be free to choose their own subject matter, but he was concerned that assimilation had rendered many incapable or afraid. Although he pointed out the very real obstacles created by the rush to assimilate, Hughes may have oversimplified the thought processes of African-American writers who did not wish to be labeled as such. As Nathan Huggins wrote forty-five years later, "one . . . must wrestle with the definition of a Negro artist; what stress should be placed on the adjective and what on the noun? Irish literature attests that this is not a peculiarly American or Negro problem" (*Harlem* 203). While African Americans like Toomer and Cullen could have regained the trust of their fellows by accepting the "Negro writer" label, the commitment of Anglo-Irish people to Ireland would always be at issue, despite the fact that Irishness was no more pure or immanent than any notion of a black race.

## Extremes of Acculturation: West Britons

The search for a coherent identity led some Irish people and African Americans in a much different direction from cultural renewal and racial uplift: they chose to emulate the dominant culture, and, if possible, to merge with it. A number of Irish people, usually middle to upper class, attempted to live as though they were English and in England, and they were often strongly criticized by Irish cultural nationalists, who contemptuously termed them "West Britons," suggesting that they considered Ireland no more than a western shire of England with no need for its own culture and language. Douglas Hyde spoke of West Britons several times in "The Necessity of De-Anglicising Ireland": he called the Anglicizing of the Irish names of people and places "West Britonizing" and stated that if Irish people do not "create a strong feeling against West Britonism," it will overwhelm them with cheap imitations of English culture, perennially six months out of date (*Language* 163, 166–67, 169). In an 1890 article entitled "Irish Writers Should Take Irish Subjects—A *Sicilian Idyll*," the young Yeats asserted that West Britons were a minority possessed of a "would-be cosmopolitanism and an actual provincialism" (*New Island* 34).

Hyde and Yeats were especially concerned that many of the cultural arbiters of Ireland preferred English culture and that their tastes were influencing the populace. Several prominent Anglo-Irish intellectuals of the time, including Edward Dowden, Robert Atkinson, and John Pentland Mahaffy, made statements that seemed to qualify them for West Briton status. They often spoke highly of English and European culture and denigrated Irish culture, suggesting that value ended abruptly at the Irish Sea. In an 1882 letter to Aubrey de Vere, Dowden stated, "I am infinitely glad that I spent my early enthusiasm on Wordsworth and Spenser and Shakespeare, and not on anything that Ireland ever produced" (184). Similarly, Mahaffy once said that his colleague Atkinson "knew the language of every country in Europe except the one he happened to be in" (qtd. in Stanford and McDowell 108). Mahaffy was not exaggerating: in addition to his command of European languages, Atkinson was conversant with Chinese, Hebrew, and Tamil, but his knowledge of and interest in the Irish language was limited to philological studies of Old and Middle Irish (Greene 6, 14–15). Both Mahaffy and Atkinson testified to the Commission on Intermediate Education in Ireland in 1899 that Irish should not be taught in the schools because the literature was either religious, ridiculous, or obscene and the language would be of no practical value to young people soon to be seeking employment.

Whether or not one was a West Briton was often a matter of judgment made by others, not a decision made by oneself. The term was often used by the more extreme cultural nationalists as a derogatory label for anyone who failed to meet their rigid standards for Irishness. The irascible D. P. Moran once wrote that "[s]ulky West Britons is the only name by which the great majority of 'nationalists' can be designated" (qtd. in Lyons 59). The most famous use of the term occurs in James Joyce's short story "The Dead," in which Molly Ivors teasingly calls Gabriel Conroy a West Briton because he reviews books for the *Daily Express,* a Unionist newspaper, and prefers to vacation on the continent rather than in

Ireland (188–90). Gabriel, a shy, apolitical man, is embarrassed by her public labeling. Joyce uses Molly and Gabriel to depict the problematic attitudes of nationalists and non-nationalists: Molly has at best a veneer of Irish culture, and Gabriel is at times ashamed of it, especially as it relates to his wife's lower-class roots in western Ireland.

One could argue as well that the label "West Briton" created too restrictive a view of Dowden, Mahaffy, and Atkinson. For instance, Dowden did not indiscriminately denigrate Irish literature: he praised works by de Vere and Yeats, and he admired the legend of Deirdre, calling it "one of the greatest tragic stories of the world" (184). Although Yeats attacked Dowden as a barrier in the path of an Irish literary revival, he agreed with many of his complaints about recent Irish literature, for example, that it often succumbed to sentiment and exaggerated the importance of Irish literary history. Likewise, Mahaffy and Atkinson were not entirely against the dissemination of Irish literature and culture: Mahaffy was among the original supporters of the Irish National Theatre in 1898, sending five pounds to Lady Gregory's subscription fund, and Atkinson devoted much of his career to editing Irish texts and creating an Irish dictionary (Stanford and McDowell 113; Greene 7).

Few were safe from suspicion of West Britonism. Yeats and even Hyde sometimes ran afoul of other cultural nationalists and acquired the label of "West Briton." While the young Yeats had termed West Britons provincials with pretensions of cosmopolitanism, the older Yeats relaxed his standards for Irishness enough to valorize the cosmopolitan and recognize that narrow-minded cultural nationalists were the true provincials. Several of the plays produced by the Irish National Theatre Society, such as *The Countess Cathleen* and *The Playboy of the Western World,* incurred nationalist wrath and cries of "West Britons" for their supposed misrepresentation of Irish people. In 1938, Hyde, cofounder of the Gaelic League and president of Ireland, found that he was not immune either: he was expelled from the Gaelic Athletic Association for attending an international soccer match in Dublin, an act that violated the association's ban on supporting non-Irish games (Dunleavy and Dunleavy 402).

### Extremes of Acculturation: Passing

The American equivalent of West Britonism is known as "passing": light-skinned African Americans with Caucasian features and a strong nerve have often chosen to cross the color line and live as white people. F. James Davis suggests that the peak years for passing were probably 1880 to 1925, when an estimated ten to twenty-five thousand people crossed the color line every year. Unlike West Britonism, in many cases, passing was temporary or occasional, or even accidental: one might pass at work or when shopping, and most did not pass permanently (22, 56). James Weldon Johnson, who spoke fluent Spanish, found that many whites in Florida assumed he was Hispanic: a number of other African Americans passed as Hispanics (*Way* 65). Several of the Harlem Renaissance authors wrote novels addressing the issue of passing, which they found both troubling and fascinating.

The character who passes is usually a pleasure-seeker, mainly interested in material concerns: like the nameless narrator in James Weldon Johnson's novel *The Autobiography of an Ex-Colored Man,* he may be fascinated with accumulating money; or, like Clare Kendry in Nella Larsen's novel *Passing,* her friends may say that she has "a having way."[10] Before they pass, these characters often perceive race as the only barrier to their happiness: like Angela Murray in Jessie Fauset's novel *Plum Bun,* they believe that if they cross the color line, their materialistic dreams will be realized.[11] The characters are often encouraged to pass by well-meaning friends of both races or have more or less accidentally passed for short periods earlier in their lives. Angela Murray's mother introduced her to passing as a social convenience (17), and the wealthy white benefactor of Johnson's narrator urged him to cross the color line as well (144–45).

When the characters first pass, they feel, as Max Disher phrases it in George Schuyler's satirical novel *Black No More,* as though "[t]he world was [their] oyster and [they] had the open sesame of a pork-colored skin!"[12] Their dreams of wealth, accomplishments, and social status finally seem attainable. They see racial prejudice expressed, as before, but now they often consider it a joke because the bigots have no idea that living refutation is at hand. At the same time, these experiences demonstrate to them that they cannot become entirely white: they remain emotionally invested in their original race. Other complications arise as well. Max Disher (28) and Larsen's Clare Kendry (145) are so bored by the white social scene that they risk being found out in order to spend time with their black friends. Johnson's narrator has to give up his plan to set ragtime and the spirituals to classical music forms (211). Fauset's Angela Murray becomes involved with a racist white man (133), and Clare Kendry marries one (171). Many of the characters fear that they will be betrayed by fathering or giving birth to a dark-skinned child.[13]

By this time, the characters have learned that being white is not the ticket to success or happiness they had imagined. Schuyler's Max Disher has trouble finding a job in his field (58), and Angela Murray envies her darker sister who is enjoying life in Harlem (209, 242). Lonely and missing a sense of racial community, the characters often stop passing or at least regret it terribly: Angela Murray retraverses the color line and becomes involved with a fellow former passer (347); Clare Kendry betrays herself by spending too much time in African-American company (238); and Johnson's narrator cannot squelch the thought that he has "sold [his] birthright for a mess of pottage" (211).

The majority of novels about passing depict it as a tempting and mysterious pursuit, but one which is basely motivated and inevitably fruitless. Henry Louis Gates says that passing is represented in literature as a Faustian "bargain with the Devil over the cultural soul" (*Colored* 24). Davis suggests that, in life, as in these novels, "[m]any found that passing was easy but that the emotional costs were high, and some therefore returned to the black community. Even during [the] peak years, the vast majority who could have passed permanently did not do so, owing to the pain of family separation, condemnation by most blacks, their fear of whites, and the loss of the security of the black community" (56–57).[14] Regardless of whether or not they presented a realistic picture of the experience of passing, by portraying it as tempting yet fruitless Harlem Renaissance writers could refute racial essentialism and valorize African-American communities at the same time. These novels assert that the difference between African and European Americans is at best skin deep, thereby invalidating notions of white superiority.[15] By depicting characters who long for their natal communities after they cross the color line, the authors showed that African Americans had an important culture to which passers might return once they had learned that, as Angela Murray phrases it, "[l]ife is more important than colour" (266).

While West Britonism and passing were both means to cross cultural barriers, they differed in several ways. Passing was usually a conscious choice available only to light-skinned African Americans, but anyone could choose to adopt English ways and the label "West Briton" could be applied to an unsuspecting Irish person in much the same manner as people today can be called "politically correct" or "incorrect" at the drop of a hat. Passing was often depicted in literature as an initially adventurous act whose adherents almost always regretted their decision. The emotions they generated in other African Americans were not entirely negative: surprise and pity were also common responses. Engendering disdain more than ambivalent fascination, West Britons do not seem to have been the subject of novelistic scrutiny to the same degree as African Americans who passed. They appeared more frequently as targets in polemical essays than as psychological studies in novels.

The title of Nella Larsen's novel *Quicksand,* which depicts the tribulations of a young woman caught between white and black society, provides a useful metaphor for African-American identity during the Harlem Renaissance. Certain kinds of racial identification were mandated by blacks and whites alike, and many individuals were caught in the resulting quagmire. Likewise, Daniel Corkery described the Irish national consciousness as "a quaking sod," which "gives no footing" (14). Both renaissances attempted to construct an identity for their people, and both endeavors were plagued with difficulties: the constructions of identity were limited and inaccurate, and those who did not fit them were often distrusted and ostracized.

# 4

# Peril of Arrogance
## The Representation of the Folk

But all representations were in some ways misrepresentations.
*Edward Hirsch*

There is peril of arrogance in the belief that one
articulates the race spirit.
*Robert Hemenway*

Because of the negative portrayals of Irish people and African Americans
in popular and high culture, both groups strove to create more positive
depictions in the arts. One of the commonplaces of Western culture and
particularly of American progressivism has been that, for better or for
worse, art possesses the power to change people. If negative images of
black and Irish people feed racist attitudes, the reasoning goes, positive
ones should help wipe them out. Many of the Harlem and Irish Renaissance writers accepted this notion and were interested in combating
oppression through literature, but they generally did not want literature
to be treated as a political tool, fearing that this would interfere with
artistic freedom and lower the quality of their work. The situation in
Ireland was further complicated by the prominence of Anglo-Irish writers
within the renaissance movement, for many Catholic nationalists did not
trust them to represent the people of Ireland.

## The Push for Propaganda

W. B. Yeats is an instructive writer to examine on this issue, for his
attitude toward it changed over the years. As a young man, Yeats

encouraged writers to use Irish themes and criticized those who chose not to. In 1890 he wrote that "[w]henever an Irish writer has strayed away from Irish themes and Irish feeling, in almost all cases he has done no more than make alms for oblivion. There is no great literature without nationality, no great nationality without literature" (*New Island* 30).[1] At this time, Yeats wanted writers not only to take up Irish themes, but also to treat their subject matter in a manner he found appropriate. For example, he criticized D. R. McAnally for using a stereotypical approach to his folklore collection *Irish Wonders* (*New Island* 91). Late in life, in a letter to the editor who collected his early essays, Yeats described the change in his beliefs about literature and propaganda:

> I knew better than I wrote. I was a propagandist and hated being one. It seems to me that I remember almost the day and hour when revising for some reprint my essay upon the Celtic movement [in "Ideas of Good and Evil"] I saw clearly the unrealities and half-truths propaganda had involved me in, and the way out. All one's life one struggles toward reality, finding always but new veils. One knows everything in one's mind. It is the words, children of the occasion, that betray. (*New Island* xviii)

Although early in his career Yeats was often unabashedly in favor of propaganda, he later adopted an intermediate position. The mature Yeats hoped that writers would choose Irish themes, but he spoke out strongly against mandating those choices. As he wrote in a 1903 theater publication, "[a] community that is opinion-ridden, even when those opinions are in themselves noble, is likely to put its creative minds into some sort of a prison. If creative minds preoccupy themselves with incidents from the political history of Ireland, so much the better, but we must not enforce them to select those incidents" (*Explorations* 115).

When younger dramatists like John Synge and Sean O'Casey aroused the ire of the nationalist and religious authorities, Yeats defended their work. He was a flexible thinker who tried to work toward two goals that often seemed at odds with each other: social change and artistic freedom. Unwilling to sacrifice the latter for the former, Yeats supported younger writers whose work often offended the Irish establishment.

In the decades before the Harlem Renaissance, a genre known as "race literature" arose in African-American writing. Its proponents argued that literature should be used by African-Americans to demonstrate the civilized and refined nature of their middle to upper classes and thereby combat white misconceptions. As the lower classes were believed to be more likely to confirm than refute racist beliefs, their appearance in literature was discouraged. During the Harlem Renaissance, writers were not altogether comfortable with race literature. The dramatist Willis Richardson acknowledged that there was a place in black literature for propaganda plays, stating in "The Hope of a Negro Drama" that "[t]hat such a work is of service will be acknowledged by anyone who will examine many of the plays of Shaw, Galsworthy and Brieux"; however, Richardson also felt that realism and the representation of the African-American folk on the stage were important and, as of yet, unexplored. He continued, "[s]till there is another kind of play; the play that shows the soul of a people" (338).

The African-American novelist Jessie Fauset was unusual in that she chose to write about bourgeois blacks yet decried limiting other writers' subject matter. Fauset felt uncomfortable with the genre known as "ghetto realism," in which writers depicted working-class black urban experiences with no holds barred: sex, alcohol, and jazz flowed along dirty streets from steamy cabarets. When W. E. B. Du Bois organized a symposium entitled "The Negro in Art: How Shall He Be Portrayed?" in 1926, Fauset wrote that the trend in younger writers toward depicting the African-American lower classes was "a grave danger making for a literary insincerity both insidious and abominable" (72). In the same piece, however, Fauset rejected the idea that African-Americans had a right to criticize black authors of ghetto realism and demand that they portray more tasteful characters. Here and elsewhere, she denounced the propaganda of race literature: as she wrote in 1924, "[t]he successful 'Negro' novel must limn Negro men and women as they really are with not only their virtues but their faults" ("New Books" 177). Fauset was on good terms with many of the practitioners of ghetto realism, including Claude McKay, who wrote in his autobiography that "[a]ll the radicals liked her, although in her social viewpoint she was away over on the other side of the fence" (*Long Way* 112). However, despite her position on race literature, many of her peers held up her work as a model for younger artists to emulate instead of suggesting, as she did, that they write about the social stratum they knew best (Wintz 152).

Given the prevalence of racial violence, the growth of the Ku Klux Klan, and the inability of the U.S. Senate to pass a federal anti-lynching bill during the 1920s, one can understand why many African-American leaders were eager to jettison artists who refused to write race literature:

they believed this genre was one of the most successful ways to change white opinions and they would brook no artistic malingering when African-American communities were in a state of emergency (Hemenway 42). As Nathan Huggins phrases it, "[e]very instance of advancement—a successful business, a new professional, a patriotic act or service—became ammunition in the barrage against arbitrary barriers. On the other hand, every failure, every crime, every black man's foolishness became a spot of shame that had to be rubbed away. Every act of a Negro that came to public attention had emotive connotations far beyond the significance of the act itself" (*Harlem* 141).

In Ireland, similar attitudes prevailed as people watched their culture being crushed beneath England's bulk while Home Rule was repeatedly rejected. Most nationalists were extremely leery of anything that might lend even the slightest credence to English prejudices. Although the Abbey Theatre had been founded with the goal of demonstrating that Irish culture was not all "buffoonery and . . . easy sentiment" (Gregory, *Theatre* 9), the work of its playwrights and of all the writers of the Irish Renaissance was under constant scrutiny. In both Ireland and black America, the renaissance writers, who were not insensitive to the needs of their people, often felt torn between the material they wished to explore and the limited range to which they were expected to conform.

Although much debate during the Irish and Harlem renaissances focused on the function of art in a movement for social change, often assuming that art has the power to alter people's beliefs, many scholars now question this assumption. David Lewis writes that his book on the Harlem Renaissance could have been subtitled "Civil Rights by Copyright" (xvi). Poet Paul Muldoon mocks Yeats's concern that his play *Cathleen Ni Houlihan* may have spurred the Easter Rising of 1916. Where Yeats, who preferred literary to literal revolution, wrote in "Man and the Echo":

> I lie wake night after night
> And never get the answers right.
> Did that play of mine send out
> Certain men the English shot? (*Poems* 345)

Muldoon opines in "7, Middagh Street":

> the answer is "Certainly not."
>
> If Yeats had saved his pencil-lead
> would certain men have stayed in bed? (134)

Although Lewis and Muldoon rightly point out a problem with the thinking of many renaissance writers, one must remember that literature is not incapable of influencing politics—one need look no further than the case of Salman Rushdie for confirmation.

## Primitivism

The belief in the power of art to change the world caused the Harlem and Irish renaissances to face pressure from within their own cultures on several issues of representation, but particularly on that of "the folk."[2] The folk might be broadly defined as the common people of a country: they usually live in rural areas, although the urban working classes and ethnic or religious minorities are sometimes treated similarly. One might more clearly define the folk as a group placed in opposition to an idea of the modern: if the modern is hurried and fragmented, for example, then the folk are peaceful and complete.[3]

The construction of the folk is part of a larger current of thought known as primitivism, pithily defined by Arthur O. Lovejoy and George Boas in 1935 as "the discontent of the civilized with civilization" (7). Valorizations of a rural or primitive existence over a sophisticated, urban life date back to Classical Greece in the Western tradition and appear in non-Western cultures as well. The trope became part of Western popular culture in the mid-eighteenth century when interpretations of Jean-Jacques Rousseau's *Discours sur l'origine et les fondemens de l'inégalité parmi les hommes* rendered his Noble Savage a symbol of the superiority of primitive life. After Rousseau, the Noble Savage appeared in many cultural guises, but, as Gaile McGregor phrases it, "his message was always the same: man could live justly and well even without the benefit of European culture and religion, if only he practiced what was natural for him" (19–20, 16). At the time of the Harlem and Irish renaissances, the folk were idealized in many industrialized cultures because of a widespread distaste among urban intellectuals and artists for the materialistic societies in which they lived. They assigned exotic and primitive qualities to the folk and thus assuaged their own world-weariness by immersing themselves where they thought they had found its opposite.

Irish primitivism grew largely out of a desire on the part of religious, political, and cultural organizations to condemn England as morally bankrupt and materialistic. In an essay on Irish folktales, Douglas Hyde said that their English cousins had been "swallowed up . . . by the waves of materialism and civilization," but the Irish tales "still surviv[ed] unengulfed on the western coasts" (*Language* 122). Hyde's comments bear out Ernest Gellner's statement that "[n]ationalism usually conquers in the name of a putative folk culture. Its symbolism is drawn from the healthy, pristine, vigorous life of the peasants" (57). In this case, spiritual and sturdy peasants, especially the women, were contrasted to a construction of English culture as weak and vulgar. Patrick Pearse once commented, "I often fancy that if some of the Old Masters had known rural Ireland, we should not have so many gross and merely earthly conceptions of the Madonna as we have" (qtd. in Foster 449).

Irish Renaissance writers often contributed to some of the prevalent notions about Irish peasants. In his account of his visits to the Aran Islands, John Synge wrote that after leaving these western islands, he experienced great distaste for the mainland town he was staying in: "[t]his town, that is usually so full of wild human interest, seems in my present mood a tawdry medley of all that is crudest in modern life. The nullity of the rich and the squalor of the poor give me the same pang of wondering disgust" (*Aran* 101). Synge detailed his preferences down to the relative merits of one Aran Island over another. Inishmaan, a more primitive island, pleased him more than Aranmore (today, Inishmore), a more modernized one, and he wrote, "the charm which the people over there [on Inishmaan] share with the birds and the flowers has been replaced here [on Aranmore] by the anxiety of men who are eager for gain" (*Aran* 125).

Occasionally he admitted that even the people of Inishmaan were not quite as picturesque as he desired: "it is only in the intonation of a few sentences or some old fragment of melody that I catch the real spirit of the island, for in general the men sit together and talk with endless iteration of the tides and fish, and of the price of kelp in Connemara" (*Aran* 49–50). Synge felt that material success would lead people to abandon their folk culture, and he was dismayed to see this effect in Aran and in other parts of western Ireland. As he wrote from the western mainland to a friend, "In a way it is all heartrending in one place the people are starving but wonderfully attractive and in another place where things are going well one has a rampant double-chinned vulgarity I haven't seen the like of" (*Letters* 117). All over the west, the folk culture seemed better preserved and the people more pleasant where prosperity had not gained a foothold.

Synge believed that modern, urban civilization alone can not produce great works of art because it is alienated from the roots of life in the countryside. In the preface to *The Playboy*, he praised Ireland for still possessing a connection to peasant culture: "[i]n Ireland, for a few years more, we have a popular imagination that is fiery and magnificent, and tender; so that those of us who wish to write start with a chance that is not given to writers where the springtime of the local life has been forgotten, and the harvest is a memory only, and the straw has been turned to bricks" (*Plays* 4).

Although in the *Playboy* preface Synge described the interaction of the folk culture and the artist as "a collaboration," the image he used for this interaction shows that he did not think of it as an equal partnership. He suggests that "when the Elizabethan dramatist took his inkhorn and sat down to his work he used many phrases that he had just heard, as he sat at dinner, from his mother or his children" (*Plays* 3). The women and children, like the people from whom Synge gathered material, can supply the phrases, but it is the artist who sits down to his work, who holds the pen. For Synge, though folk cultures had the power to revitalize a vitiated urban artist, they were not equally artistic.

However, the writers' attitudes toward primitivism are not always easy to discern. Yeats, for example, is often criticized for holding primitivist views, but his writings show that he perceived quite clearly the origins of and some of the problems with primitivism. In 1892, he humorously described the prevalent reaction to urban materialism: "[t]he cultivated man has begun a somewhat hectic search for the common pleasures of common men and for the rough accidents of life. The typical young poet of our day is an aesthete with a surfeit, searching sadly for his lost Philistinism, his heart full of an unsatisfied hunger for the commonplace. He is an Alastor tired of his woods and longing for beer and skittles" (*Island* 59). Especially early in his career, Yeats's forays into primitivism were frequently engendered by his desire to link his occult and literary beliefs. Since the young Yeats felt that Irish writers ought to use Irish subjects, he had to make his interest in spiritualism an Irish quality. Thus, in an 1886 review, he wrote that the "love of shadowy Hy Brasil is very characteristic of the Celtic race, ever desiring the things that lie beyond the actual" (qtd. in Marcus 22). Similarly, in his 1893 collection of stories and sketches entitled *The Celtic Twilight*, he described a man named Paddy Flynn, who "was indeed always cheerful, though," says Yeats, "I thought I could see in his eyes . . . a melancholy which was well-nigh a portion of their joy; the visionary melancholy of purely instinctive natures and of all animals" (3–4). By asserting that Irish people were visionary and spiritual, Yeats was able to connect his two interests and preserve his belief system.

Despite his use of primitivism to justify his interest in the occult, Yeats remained aware that Ireland was "a country where the Gaelic League has created a preoccupation with the countryman" (*Explorations* 182). He was sometimes critical of the League and other language movements in Europe, which he described in a 1906 theater publication as "attempting . . . to restore a more picturesque way of life." "The life of the villages," he wrote, "with its songs, its dances and its pious greetings . . . grows more noble as he [the language enthusiast] meditates upon it, for it mingles with the Middle Ages until he can no longer see it as it is" (*Explorations* 205). Although Yeats constructed Irish peasants for his own ends, he also perceived others' forays into primitivism. As somewhat of an outsider to the Celtic Irish culture, the Anglo-Irish Yeats may have had an advantage in assessing such emotional subjects objectively.

In America, primitivism developed largely from popular psychology rather than politics. The theories of Freud and his contemporaries led many intellectuals to "deny the artifices of civility and manner and to seek the true self through spontaneity and the indulgence of impulse" (Huggins, *Harlem* 7). African Americans, especially the black folk, had long been considered simple, emotional people, and intellectuals, both black and white, turned to them as a source of the spontaneity and simplicity which they felt could revitalize their vitiated culture. Although anthropologists like Franz Boas had been suggesting for thirty years that so-called primitive cultures were actually complex and diverse, popular intellectual culture clung to primitivism (Torgovnick 19). In her autobiography *Dust Tracks on a Road,* Zora Neale Hurston recounts a typical evening at the home of her patron, Mrs. Charlotte Osgood Mason: "[t]here she was sitting up there at the table over capon, caviar and gleaming silver, eager to hear every word on every phase of life on a saw-mill 'job.' I must tell the tales, sing the songs, do the dances, and repeat the raucous sayings and doings of the Negro farthest down. She is altogether in sympathy with them, because she says truthfully they are utterly sincere in living" (177). Mrs. Mason had been interested in cultures like those of the Plains Indians and the African-American folk for many years, and the Harlem Renaissance gave her the opportunity to serve as a patron for several artists. She was a strong-willed individual, however, and she attempted to control the work of the writers whom she assisted. If they deviated from the tenets of primitivism, she was displeased. She told Harvard-educated Alain Locke to "slough off white culture—using it only to clarify the thoughts that surge in your being" (qtd. in Lewis 154). As another of her "godchildren," Langston Hughes, stated: "[s]he wanted me to be primitive and know and feel the intuitions of the primitive. But, unfortunately, I did not feel the rhythms of the primitive surging through me, and so I could not live and write as though I did" (*Big Sea* 325).[4] Patrons and publishers, among others, pressured black writers to behave like and write about members of an idealized folk culture.

As in the Irish movement, many members of the Harlem Renaissance accepted aspects of primitivism. In a letter to Hughes, Hurston related her plan for a "*real* Negro theatre": "we shall act out the folk tales, however short, with the abrupt angularity and naivete of the primitive 'bama Nigger" (qtd. in Gates, "Tragedy" 9). The desire for assimilation among many middle-class blacks angered Hurston, and she hoped to create a theater that would show the value of black folk culture; despite the fact that she came from a rural Southern background, however, her own view of the African-American folk was often informed by primitivism.

James Weldon Johnson was in some ways a more typical black primitivist than Hurston, because he believed—while she did not—that in order for folk culture to be considered artistic, it would have to be mediated by high cultural forms. The dichotomy inherent in primitivism between the urban and the rural helped split art into two types, high and low, in the minds of many people, including John Synge. They felt that folk culture was the raw material for high art, but that it was not in itself truly artistic.

In the preface to his anthology *The Book of American Negro Poetry*, Johnson called ragtime, the blues, spirituals, the cakewalk, and folk tales "lower forms of art." Although he claimed that "they are evidence of a power that will some day be applied to the higher forms," and although he stated that he was deeply moved by the beauty of the spirituals, Johnson clearly classified African-American folk culture productions as low art (xv). The best that he could say of them is that "there is frequently revealed a flash of real, primitive poetry." At worst, he wrote, "the lines themselves are often very trite" (xvii). Johnson applied the values of high Western culture to the spirituals and, not surprisingly, found them lacking.

Later in this same preface, Johnson suggested that black writers should follow the example of John Synge and create "a form that is freer and larger than dialect, but which will still hold the racial flavor" (xli). Johnson took his own advice in *God's Trombones,* a collection of African-American sermons put into verse form. In his autobiography, Johnson discussed how he came to write this work:

> I had long been planning that at some time I should take the primitive stuff of the old-time Negro sermon and, through art-governed expression, make it into poetry. I felt that this primitive stuff could be used in a way similar to that in which a composer makes use of a folk theme in writing a major composition. I believed that the characteristic qualities . . . could be preserved and, at the same time, the composition as a whole be enlarged beyond the circumference of mere race, and given universality. (*Way* 335)

Johnson felt it was important to lift folk art out of its context and make it part of high art. Hurston commented acidly on a similar attitude in a letter to Thomas E. Jones, the president of Fisk University, in 1934: "it was thought that no Negro vocalist was an artist unless he or she could take good Negro music and turn it into mediocre white sounds" (qtd. in Hemenway 204).

Like Hurston, many writers are less easy to classify than Johnson. Claude McKay, for example, often wavered between denouncing and practicing primitivism. It would be reductive to say that he participated without reservation in the primitivist depictions of African Americans; however, his work does provide some remarkable examples of that genre. In a scene from his first novel, *Home to Harlem,* he describes the transformation of materialistic prostitutes into passionate dancers: "The women, carried away by the sheer rhythm of delight, had risen above their commercial instincts (a common trait of Negroes in emotional states) and abandoned themselves to pure voluptuous jazzing" (58). McKay's second novel, *Banjo,* continued to follow the primitivist line to such a degree that the editor of the *Nation,* Freda Kirchwey, compared his philosophy to that of groups espousing white supremacy: "He shares with his brothers of the Klan a dangerous proclivity to generalize—only he reverses the values" (614).

McKay also acceded to primitivism in his depictions of Jamaican peasants, although in a different way. He had left home in 1912, never to return—except in his poetry, where he often celebrated the land of his childhood, creating a bucolic landscape peopled with idealized peasants.

For example, in his 1921 poem "My Mother," McKay described the land around his mother's grave: "The older folk are at their peaceful toil, / Some pulling up the weeds, some plucking corn, / And others breaking up the sun-baked soil" (*Poems* 22). McKay creates an idyllic scene by using the adjective "peaceful" before giving details—the difficult labor of weeding, harvesting, and plowing. As a young man living in Jamaica, his poetry tended to be a less-idealized depiction of peasant life, depicting the problems caused by the Jamaican color-based caste system.[5] In "The Apple-Woman's Complaint," a poem from his 1912 collection, *Constab Ballads,* McKay portrays a street vendor angry that her trade has been suddenly outlawed: "Ef me no wuk, me boun' fe tief; / S'pose dat will please de pólice chief!" She clearly states the inequities of the system:

> Black nigger wukin' laka cow
> An' wipin' sweat-drops from him brow,
> Dough him is dyin' sake o' need,
> P'lice an' dem headman boun' fe feed. (*Dialect* 57)

By juxtaposing the phrases "boun' fe tief" and "boun' fe feed," McKay shows the inevitable outcome: the apple woman will turn to crime to survive as surely as the police and the headman will feast at night.

Although his depictions of Jamaican peasants and African Americans were sometimes affected by primitivism, McKay was able to detect and reject similar types of constructions. For example, although he was involved in socialist organizations, he could separate the working classes from the myths generated about them. As he wrote in a letter to H. L. Mencken, "[s]horn of propaganda and romance the workers individually are not better to me than other people, but it happens that their social status gives reformers and agitators their weapon against opponents" (qtd. in Cooper, *Rebel* 196). Though he could have made similar claims about primitivism and the folk, McKay's comments on that subject were rarely so trenchant. For example, he wrote in his autobiography that, "[f]or all their knowledge and sophistication, [his white fellow expatriates] couldn't understand the instinctive and animal and purely physical pride of a black person resolute in being himself and yet living a simple civilized life like themselves. Because their education in their white world had trained them to see a person of color either as an inferior or as an exotic" (*Long Way* 245). Even as he condemned the mindset that encouraged whites to "see a person of color either as an inferior or as an exotic," he used words such as "instinctive," "animal," and "physical" to describe black people.[6] McKay, like Hurston and Yeats, was caught up in the mindset of primitivism even as he rejected aspects of it. Primitivism is usually associated with hegemonic cultures' views of subordinate groups, but black and Irish writers often accepted and promulgated its tenets.

## Ambivalence

While intellectuals at the time of the Irish and Harlem renaissances were often passionately interested in the folk, many middle-class Irish people and African Americans were ambivalent about or uncomfortable with folk culture. Urban, middle-class Irish people often were not comfortable about the peasants in their cultural or familial background. Since, like many African Americans, they had recently moved to urban areas, "New Dubliners" often tried to assimilate to the dominant culture and so were loath to admit a peasant background. A number of them were also nationalists, however, and they therefore joined in the Gaelic League's idealization of peasants (Hirsch 1123). These contradictory impulses rendered them more ambivalent than their African-American counterparts, who were often outright negative about their folk origins. Desmond Fennell connects this ambivalence to the widespread feeling that the Irish language and peasant culture were antithetical to material success; thus, "we could only wish sentimentally for an Irish revival, make guilt-ridden and uncoordinated gestures in that direction, and employ Irish as a shibboleth in our revolutionary state building" (75).

In addition to these conflicting feelings, middle-class Dubliners of peasant background were often also distressed by the very use of the word "peasant" by organizations like the Gaelic League and the Abbey Theatre: it had a negative connotation and it was not how the rural poor would have referred to themselves in the first place (MacLochlainn 19–20). Conor Cruise O'Brien suggests that the Irish National Theatre Society's first production, Yeats's *Countess Cathleen,* would thus have shocked some people not only because of the religious issues it raised, but also because it portrayed "peasants," a term which he calls "virtually taboo" among the new urban middle class (60).

African Americans often considered folk culture a legacy of the days of slavery, best forgotten and certainly not celebrated. In his 1932 novel *Infants of the Spring,* Wallace Thurman depicted a singer who refuses to perform spirituals, saying, "I'm no slave, and I won't sing slave music" (108). The character considered folk culture inartistic and an embarrassment to the cultivated African American. Characters in novels were not the only people who felt this way: Carolyn Wedin Sylvander suggests that Jessie Fauset was much more comfortable with African than with African-American folk materials because collections of the latter often used dialect, which she did not like. In a 1923 review of Ambrose E. Gonzales's compilation *The Black Border: Gullah Stories of the Carolina Coast*, Fauset wrote that "[o]nly the philologist or the sociologist will take the time to wade through this mass of unrecognizable, unpronounceable dialect" ("Notes" 164).

Even if black people were interested in folk culture, rising in social class could quickly cut them off from it. In Hurston's novel *Their Eyes Were Watching God*, new mayor Joe Starks forbids his wife Janie to listen to the tale-telling on the porch of his general store. Referring to her social position, he says, "Ah can't see what uh woman uh yo' sability would want tuh be treasurin' all dat gumgrease from folks dat don't even own de house dey sleep in" (85). The folk could be adopted by urban intellectuals, and their culture could reinforce a sense of identity, but to those who wished to prove their sophistication, folk culture often seemed a liability. As sociologist Charles Johnson explained in *The New Negro*, "[t]he generation in whom lingered memories of the painful degradation of slavery could not be expected to cherish even those pearls of song and poetry born of suffering. They would be expected to do just as they did: rule out the Sorrow Sings as the product of ignorant slaves, taboo dialect as incorrect English, and the priceless folklore as the uncultured expression of illiterates,—an utterly conscious effort to forget the past" (297). Johnson believed that the current generation was slowly beginning to appreciate African-American folk culture, but he acknowledged that many were still not comfortable with it.

### Effects on the Writers

Because "the folk" was a contested and emotional term, the writers of the Harlem and Irish renaissances faced criticism from several quarters. The issues explored in their work often triggered fears that they would feed the dominant cultures' assumptions about their peoples, and indeed the English and white American audiences pushed for primitivist depictions. Many African-American power brokers wanted only portrayals of the middle to upper classes, considering literature about the working classes or the rural folk to be dangerous. In Ireland, one did have the option of writing about the peasantry, but another set of restrictions applied: religious and nationalist forces required that they be depicted as pure and noble. Writers in both movements were similarly constrained from writing openly about sexuality: not only was it largely considered a distasteful subject, but it was thought to have great potential for feeding the prejudices of English people and white Americans, who often fed on stories of the size of Irish families and of the sexual proclivities of African-Americans. In addition to class and moral standards, there were also political tests: in Ireland, one could suffer for being too nationalistic or not sufficiently so; and in America, black writers had to be wary of how such issues as self-defense, miscegenation, and assimilation would be perceived by both black and white elites. Handled indelicately, any one of these issues could ruin one's career—or endanger one's life. The artists of both movements frequently found themselves navigating between the Scylla of political responsibility and the Charybdis of artistic freedom.[7]

While many well-to-do black people wanted to see only their own classes depicted in literature, powerful nationalist and religious forces in Ireland expected the Irish Renaissance to write about the folk. Their concerns about the propriety of those representations, however, were just as strong as those of the black communities. John Synge's plays were the subject of a number of attacks. In October 1902, his first play to be produced, *In the Shadow of the Glen,* drew criticism from the nationalist journalist Arthur Griffith, who called it a slander on Irish peasant women based not on Irish life but on the ancient Greek story of the Widow of Ephesus. Griffith wrote, "Synge is pandering to the enemies of Ireland. . . . Synge, who is utterly a stranger to the Irish character as any Englishman, has yet denigrated us for the enlightenment of his countrymen" (qtd. in O'Connor 236). Synge, who was fascinated by connections between Irish peasant culture and mainland European culture, was furious. But the public reaction in 1907 to *The Playboy* was even worse. The *Freeman's Journal* said of its characters that "No adequate idea can be given of the barbarous jargon, the elaborate and incessant cursings of these repulsive creatures" (qtd. in Greene and Stephens 257). This was *after* a number of cuts had been made in rehearsal. The social forces behind reviews like these exerted considerable pressure on Irish writers to conform to strict nationalist and Catholic notions of the peasants.

African-American writers could be attacked merely for writing about the folk—or not writing about them. Langston Hughes's second volume of poems, *Fine Clothes to the Jew,* published in February 1927, contained many vignettes of working-class black life.[8] Hughes had worked at a laundry in Washington, D.C., during the winter of 1924–25, and he had spent a great deal of time with the black poor of the city during his fourteen months in residence (Berry 57–58). Although the publications of national African-American organizations like the NAACP's *Crisis* and the Urban League's *Opportunity* reviewed his collection favorably, some major black newspapers printed excoriating reviews. The *Amsterdam News* headline read "Langston Hughes—the Sewer Dweller" (22). Particularly offensive were the poems which addressed the lives of black prostitutes, such as "Red Silk Stockings":

> Put on yo' red silk stockings,
> Black gal.
> Go out an' let de white boys
> Look at yo' legs. (*Poems* 122)

Hughes fought back in the *Pittsburgh Courier,* another black newspaper that had printed an unfavorable review. In two articles published in April 1927, he answered the criticisms of his book and lashed out at the African-American middle and upper classes for wanting writers to depict only respectable black people (*Bad,* 1, 8).[9] But the distaste for portrayals of the seamier side of life ran deep. Distinguished black critic Benjamin Brawley wrote in 1937 that "it would have been just as well, perhaps better, if the book had never been published. No other ever issued reflects more fully the abandon and the vulgarity of its age" (*Genius* 248).

While depicting the lives of working-class African Americans could get a writer in trouble with the black bourgeoisie, the white literary establishment was simultaneously encouraging black people to write about the folk. In 1922 Sherwood Anderson told Jean Toomer that he was afraid "intense white men" would influence his style and "spoil him," and he urged Toomer to retain the primitivist aspects of his work. At the same time, novelist Waldo Frank tried to steer Toomer away from writing about urban African Americans and toward exploring the culture of rural Southern black people. "Keep yourself warm underneath," he wrote, "in the soil, where the throb is" (qtd. in Kerman and Eldridge 86). At first, Toomer accepted the advice of primitivists like Anderson and Frank, but eventually he grew interested in other subjects and impatient with narrow views of what his style and theme should be. He was more interested in racial synthesis than in the reputed elements of an individual race. Toomer and Hughes both found that "the folk" was a highly contested construct, whether or not one chose to write about them.

Since the Harlem and Irish renaissances ended, scholars have criticized many of the writers for their portrayals of the folk; ironically, they often suggest that the writers obediently followed the dictates of primitivism, whereas their contemporaries often felt they could have followed those dictates more closely.[10] For many writers, completely avoiding primitivism proved an impossible task: American publishers often encouraged writers to essentialize their black characters, and the peasants were too deeply invested with cultural meaning for most Irish writers to avoid constructing them for their own use. Edward Hirsch's comment about Irish peasants holds true for the African-American folk as well: "[t]he country people were important . . . not for their own sake but because of what they signified as a concept" (1118).

# Conclusion

# Affirmative Actions
## Implications for Literary Studies

> [It is] an isolationist, group-by-group approach that emphasizes
> "authenticity" and cultural heritage within the individual,
> somewhat idealized group—at the expense of more widely
> shared historical conditions and cultural features, of
> dynamic interaction and syncretism.
>
> *Werner Sollors*

In the preceding chapters I have discussed several of the elements shared by the Harlem and Irish renaissances—historical conditions as well as problems of language, identity, and representation, especially the representation of the folk—and shown that comparisons of the two literatures were not uncommon earlier in this century, especially in America. In recent years, the comparisons have continued and the Irish side has expanded greatly.

In the last thirty years, Irish political organizations in particular have picked up on the black-Irish connection. During the late 1960s, the Northern Ireland Civil Rights Association (NICRA) was formed by Catholics dissatisfied with both the Unionist government and the nationalist opposition. As John Darby notes, "The strategies of NICRA borrowed heavily from pacifist non-violent techniques which had been tested elsewhere, especially in North America—sit-ins, processions, songs and publications—all conducted in full view of television cameras and pressmen" (104). "We Shall Overcome" was a favorite on NICRA marches. On a more radical note, C. L. Innes heard Stokely Carmichael and Conor

Cruise O'Brien compare Black Power and Sinn Fein at a symposium in 1965 (5). According to Bill Rolston, wall murals in Belfast have also compared black South African and Northern Irish struggles against colonialism (23).

In addition to political borrowings, artists have also suggested similarities between Irish and black people today. In an interview with Richard Kearney, the Irish musician Bono of the group U2 listed the blues and gospel music among his band's influences and compared the Irish and black quests for identity (189–90). The novel and film *The Commitments* explored the influence of soul music on an Irish band of the same name. As one character says, "[t]he Irish are the niggers of Europe, lads. . . . Say it loud, I'm black and I'm proud" (Doyle 9). The inability of "The Commitments" to finally commit to soul music is a poignantly ironic example of how the problematic aspects of cross-cultural comparisons continue today as well.

The black-Irish connection also continues to be drawn in America. In 1992, Maya Angelou said that she would like to see her play *And Still I Rise* performed with an Irish cast. The following year, Nerys and Orlando Patterson published an essay in *The New York Times* entitled "St. Patrick Was a Slave" (A19). The Trinidadian writer Mustapha Matura's adaptation of Synge, entitled *Playboy of the West Indies,* was performed in New York's Lincoln Center the same year (Rich B1).

These events are, however, not always welcome today among African Americanists. Many of these scholars are interested in the building of a canon of black literature, which often means restricting oneself to the study of internal influences. As Henry Louis Gates puts it, "When I was a student in the 1960's, my professors still thought of the great American tradition as white and male. . . . Then, from the late 1960's on, some of us began to analyze a self-contained black tradition as a corrective" (Winkler A7). After I gave a paper on interracial literary influence at the National Association of African-American Studies (NAAAS) conference in 1994, some of the younger black participants told me afterward that despite their interest in the subject, they felt threatened by my paper because they did not feel that African Americans had finished building a canon of their own. Aijaz Ahmad testifies that this is not a particularly black phenomenon:

The axiomatic fact about *any* canon formation, even when it initially takes shape as a counter-canon, is that when a period is

defined and homogenized, or the desired literary typology is constructed, the canonizing agency selects certain kinds of authors,
texts, styles, and criteria of classification and judgement, privileging
them over others which may also belong in the same period, arising
out of the same space of production, but which manifestly fall
outside the principles of inclusion enunciated by that self-same
agency. (123)

As time passes and canons are built, more African Americanists will
feel comfortable exploring interracial literary interaction. Unfortunately,
another obstacle stands in the way of this cross-cultural approach to
literature: identity politics, the belief in the preeminence of affiliative
connections such as gender and race.[1] Identity politics often leads to
unfounded assumptions about people's abilities and interests: all Asian-
American women will study Maxine Hong Kingston; an African American is wrong to study Greek history; a white person cannot truly compre-
hend nonwhite literature. Daphne Patai muses, "I have often wondered
how soon it will be before someone suggests that my 'identity' (North
American) should cause me to cease teaching classes in one of my areas of
research, Brazilian women" (B2). Ann duCille says that "the field of
African-American studies is often treated like a black ghetto—like the
one right and proper place for black intellectuals" ("Occult" 604). I have
been asked several times if I am Irish, as though that would explain
exactly why I have undertaken this project. But as Gates phrases it, "the
fundamental premise of the academy is that all things ultimately are
knowable; all are therefore teachable. What would we say to a person
who said that we couldn't teach Milton because we are not Anglo-Saxon,
or male, or heterosexual—or blind!" (*Canons* 127).[2]

Identity politics affects the work of both white and black scholars: for
example, white African Americanists often feel the need to justify their
research interests. John Callahan spends much of the first chapter of his
book *In the African-American Grain* talking about the African Americans he met while growing up in New Haven, as though he must conjure
his way to an insider status. As Callahan puts it at the end of his
autobiographical narrative, "maybe by telling you a little of who I'm for,
I am better able to tell you what I'm for" (23). But Callahan's narrative
recounts a succession of failures, misunderstandings, and unfortunate
silences. Where, then, does it place him? Similarly, Barbara Johnson
begins her essay "Thresholds of Difference: Structures of Address in Zora

Neale Hurston" in a coyly tentative manner: "It was not clear to me what I, a white deconstructor, was doing talking about Zora Neale Hurston, a black novelist and anthropologist, or to whom I was talking. . . . It was as though I were asking Zora Neale Hurston for answers to questions I did not even know I was unable to formulate" (172). Callahan and Johnson suffer from the extreme self-consciousness of the white African Americanist in the age of identity politics. They, and others like them, have been told, variously, that they cannot fully understand African-American literature, that they are merely dilettantes or scavengers, and that they must acknowledge their complicity in a racist culture. No wonder that Hurston biographer Robert Hemenway says that the definitive work on this author will be written by a black woman (xx).[3] I have written my conclusion on this subject not because I feel that I must justify my research interests, but because I believe that these issues should be raised to encourage further cross-cultural studies and to expose the discouraging of such work.

Black scholars are also affected by identity politics; as I have suggested, the internal model of literary influence is flawed but very attractive. It arises from a very positive experience—the joy of discovering one's African-American literary antecedents, both recent ones and those long ago.[4] Records of this joy date back at least to early anthologies of African-American literature published in the mid-nineteenth century. W. E. B. Du Bois's 1903 publication of *The Souls of Black Folk* provides an excellent example: many African Americans felt upon reading this book that they had found a soulmate, someone of their race who eloquently articulated their feelings. Claude McKay wrote in his autobiography that "[t]he book shook me like an earthquake. Dr. Du Bois stands on a pedestal illuminated in my mind" (*Long Way* 110). Similarly, Langston Hughes stated that "[m]y earliest memory of any book at all, except a schoolbook, is *The Souls of Black Folk* by Du Bois (*Fight* 203).

With the advent of a more positive racial identification in the 1960s, more young African Americans began to be exposed to works of literature by members of their own race. As these young people matured, a number of them followed academic or literary careers, and when they published books of their own, writer after writer spoke of his or her first experience with an African-American literary tradition. Novelist Terry McMillan wrote in the introduction to *Breaking Ice: An Anthology of Contemporary African-American Fiction* that "[a]s a child, I didn't know that African-American people wrote books." Even as a college student in the early 1970s anticipating the first day of a class called Afro-American Literature, McMillan wondered, "[d]id *we* really have enough writers to warrant an entire class?" (xv, xvi). In *In Search Of Our Mothers' Gardens*, Alice Walker related how her discovery of Zora Neale Hurston's folklore collection *Mules and Men* saved her own African-American folklore project from oblivion in 1970: Walker had found that most African-American folklore had been collected by whites whose presentation of the material reflected their racial biases. When she found Hurston's work mentioned in a footnote, she tracked it down and discovered what she termed "a model," and a "perfect book," the source without which her own work would never have been written (12, 84). Walker's idealization of Hurston results in part from the lack of an African-American literary tradition in her youth.

Thus, only a short while ago, the discovery of African-American literature often came relatively late in life and meant the unveiling of a new horizon; however, a new generation of writers and scholars is arriving, those who were born as the first black literature classes sprang onto course schedules across the country and who insisted that they were old enough to stay up for *Roots,* to read *The Color Purple.* Because they have matured after a literary revolution, this new generation of scholars must think critically about the meaning of an African-American literary tradition, must develop the revolution into a stable and wise government, for they risk the rigidity that often follows revolution. Literary influence must be treated as a phenomenon capable of being either internal or external, and scholars must not assume they know how black writers feel about the subject.

Here is Countee Cullen, Harlem Renaissance poet, explaining why he subtitled his collection *Caroling Dawn* "an anthology of verse by Negro writers" and not "an anthology of Negro verse": "As heretical as it may sound, there is the probability that Negro poets, dependent as they are on the English language, may have more to gain from the rich background of English and American poetry than from any nebulous atavistic yearnings towards an African inheritance" (xi). Because the literary traditions available to Cullen's authors consisted almost exclusively of "English and American poetry," the writers were always already more than "Negro poets." Their poetic education placed them in a Western tradition, even if their racial education did not. And rejecting an "African inheritance" did not render Cullen an unracial poet: many of his poems address racial themes, though they reflect an English and European-American poetic sensibility.

Like Cullen, Langston Hughes accepted external literary influence. In *The Big Sea*, he spoke of the writers who were his adolescent enthusiasms: "I think it was [Guy] de Maupassant who made me really want to be a writer and write stories about Negroes, so true that people in faraway lands would read them—even after I was dead" (34). Hughes did not see any contradiction between being influenced by de Maupassant and writing "stories about Negroes"; in fact, his interest in the French writer showed him that a writer could have an international appeal. The boy who read de Maupassant became the creator of a blues voice in African-American poetry: his eclectic reading did not hinder his racial agenda.

References to external influence by African-American writers continued to occur after the advent of racial pride and the Black Arts movement, which stressed an African-American literary tradition. For example, in a 1977 interview, poet Robert Hayden described the effect of reading George Eliot and Nathaniel Hawthorne as follows: "I loved those books, partly because they took me completely out of the environment that I lived in, and they appealed to my imagination, because they were full of strange and wonderful things that I'd had no direct experience with" (93). Although Hayden read African-American literature with great pleasure, he also acknowledged that British and European-American literature were important and exciting to him. Reading about people like oneself has been emphasized in the last twenty-five years, but Hayden reminds us that reading about people unlike oneself is also valuable. Like Cullen, Hayden did not wish to be called a "Negro poet"—he found the appellation inaccurate and narrowing—but also like Cullen, he was deeply concerned with racial issues.

David Bradley, a contemporary novelist, shares some of the older writers' beliefs about literary influence and traditions. In an interview published in *Callaloo*, Bradley said, "I never, ever, knew what James Stewart meant when he said, "we have to use black models." I never could figure out what a black model was. All I ever knew was that Africans did not write novels. So, if you're going to write a novel, you're inevitably dealing with a European form" (Blake and Miller 35). Like Cullen, Bradley acknowledges that the notion of a purely African-American tradition, a "black model," is suspect because African-American writing is informed by European and European-American literature as well as by African and African-American literary traditions.

Despite the obstacle of identity politics, literary critics have begun to pick up on what many writers have been saying all along and to examine interracial literary interactions. In her 1992 work, *Playing in the Dark: Whiteness and the Literary Imagination,* Toni Morrison states that "[t]he contemplation of [the] black presence [in American literature] is central to any understanding of our national literature and should not be permitted to hover at the margins of the literary imagination" (5). Works by Shelley Fisher Fishkin, Ann duCille, George Hutchinson, Aldon L. Nielsen, Eric Sundquist, and Kenneth Warren, to mention a few, also address this issue. In an article in the *Chronicle of Higher Education,* Fishkin states that "[l]iterary criticism has been segregated. The assumption has been that white texts grew out of a white tradition, black texts out of a black tradition. . . . The implication is that we need to pay more attention to African-American culture, even when we study the canon. By the same token, we have to be aware of the influence of canonical works on African-American writers" (Winkler A7).

Identity politics means placing inordinate importance on certain of the characteristics that make up our identities; in doing so, we widen the gaps between groups and lessen the chances for peaceful coexistence. If we are to study literature well, much less live together, we must recognize our ability to cross boundaries of identity, for they are more porous than we know, less rigid than some would have us believe.

# Notes

## Preface

1. My source, David Artis, referred to the "Carolina Players." I have been unable to locate a group by this name. Artis may have been referring to the Carolina Playmakers, a white theater troupe that performed folk plays, including some about the black folk. Their director, Frederick Koch, and their Pulitzer Prize–winning playwright Paul Green were influenced by the Abbey Theatre. Some Harlem Renaissance writers, including Zora Neale Hurston and Langston Hughes, visited the all-white University of North Carolina to meet with Koch and Green. I have not been able to find records of a black theater troupe in the state during the Harlem Renaissance, though the North Carolina Negro Dramatic Association was founded in 1933.

2. See also Hatch, ed., *Black Theater, U.S.A.*, 209.

3. In her essay "Mr. Bennett and Mrs. Brown," Woolf wrote that "in or about December, 1910, human character changed." Her specificity was facetious, but her point is ordinarily well-taken.

## Introduction: "How Black Sees Green and Red"

1. Allen argues that Irish immigrants underwent a transformation from oppressed to oppressors, from sympathizing with black people to being prejudiced against them. He gives the striking example of John Hughes, first archbishop of New York, who published an antislavery poem shortly after emigrating to the United States, yet became a prominent apologist for slavery later in life (168–69).

2. The boycott was sparked by a Limerick priest, Father John Creagh, who spread rumors of blood libel—the alleged killing of Christian children for their blood.

3. Hurston, *Moses,* xxi-xxii. All future references are to this edition. Hurston had heard some of these stories while traveling in the West Indies, and she documented them in *Tell My Horse,* a folklore travelogue.

4. Although Zoe does not fit the "darkey" stereotype, she is one of the first stage incarnations of the "tragic mulatto."

5. Gibbons notes that comparisons of Irish people and Native Americans date back to 1562 (98).

6. L. Curtis points out that many European countries had a group of people— often an ethnic, religious, or political minority—called "white Negroes" or "simianized men." See *Apes and Angels,* 13–14.

7. See, for example, Walton, "Using the Real Thing." He argues that the new trend of using African-American actors to play black roles should continue.

8. A glance at Hill's index reveals numerous references to Ireland and Irish politics in Garvey's speeches.

9. See Cooper, *Rebel Sojourner,* 12, 18, for a description of McKay's complex class status.

### Chapter 1: Waking from the Nightmare

1. Most Americans are not familiar with the colonialist meaning of the term "plantation," which the *Oxford English Dictionary* traces back to 1586. The two meanings of the term provide an interesting nexus of the racial and the colonial.

2. Beckett notes that in 1628 the Gaelic Irish gentry still used the Irish language exclusively enough for some of them to request an Irish-speaking judge.

3. By dichotomizing Irish and English, the English helped create Irish nationalism, for Irish people had little sense of national unity beforehand.

4. Genovese points out, however, that some communication across linguistic barriers did occur, especially when slaves were kept at coastal shipment areas long enough to learn pidgin versions of European languages. See *Roll, Jordan, Roll,* 432.

5. I am indebted to Foster, *Modern Ireland,* 154, 205–11, and Fallis, *Irish Renaissance,* 21–22, for the following information on the Penal Laws. South Africa's approach to minority rule for most of the twentieth century provides an instructive modern comparison.

6. Sowell adds, "It is unnecessary to attempt to say who was worse off on net balance. The mere fact that such a comparison could be made indicates something of the desperate poverty of Irish peasants in the 1830s."

7. With more recent sources at his disposal, Foster suggests a higher Irish immigration rate (1,500,000) than does Sowell, but Foster's statistics are not limited to immigration to United States. Regardless, much movement occurred in both populations. See Foster, *Modern Ireland,* 324.

8. See Fallis, *Irish Renaissance,* 56, and Lyons, *Culture,* 27–28. Fallis approvingly quotes a similar passage by Yeats, and Lyons cites this one with only chronological reservations.

9. "If We Must Die" also circulated among African-American inmates at Attica State Prison during the 1971 riots. See Cooper, *Rebel Sojourner,* 101.

10. Gregory mentions receiving a letter (apparently lost) from Synge with these words in 1904.

11. Harlem Renaissance writers also explored their cultural roots, including Africa, the Caribbean, and the South, but Harlem had a special place in their imaginations that Dublin did not for Irish Renaissance writers (Hale, personal communication).

12. A Unionist newspaper was one which supported the Union with England, not a Labour paper.

13. The title of Van Vechten's novel is slang for the balcony of a theater in which African-American patrons were seated: it encapsulates the ambiguity inherent in Harlem, where African Americans could enjoy a sense of community, but in appalling conditions enforced by racial discrimination.

14. Archer points out that the two organizations were not completely at odds: the IRB and the IPP worked together on a number of occasions in the second half of the nineteenth century. See "Necessary Ambiguity," 30.

### Chapter 2: Collaboration, Isolation, and Conflict

1. Atkinson and Mahaffy will be discussed shortly.

2. Heaney's essay was originally delivered as a speech the previous year. See also Bhabha, "Of Mimicry and Men," 125–33, and Baker, "Caliban's Triple Play," 190–96.

3. The founders of the theater movement were not ignorant of the importance of producing plays in Irish, nor were they unwilling. Just as Harlem Renaissance theaters had trouble finding plays by African-American authors, Irish-language plays were difficult to come by in fin de siècle Ireland.

4. In a letter to Yeats quoted in D. Murphy, 9. Lady Gregory reiterated her motivation in the end notes to *Gods and Fighting Men,* 462.

5. Compare Kinsella's version, p. 27 with Gregory, *Cuchulain,* 26. Both mention Cúchulain looking at Emer's breasts, but Kinsella also has a phallic joke in the scene.

6. By 1913 Pearse had changed his mind about Synge, but many Gaelic Leaguers continued to despise his work.

7. Dunbar also wrote many poems in dialects other than African-American, including Hoosier, German-American, and Irish-American vernaculars.

8. See, for example, the hostile accounts of Lawson, *Dunbar Critically Examined,* 78, and Okeke-Ezigbo, "Paul Laurence Dunbar," 481–96.

9. Dunbar, *Complete Poems,* 138. All future references are to this edition.

10. The section of *Roll, Jordan, Roll* entitled "De Good Massa" bears reading.

11. Hemenway, *Zora Neale Hurston,* is an invaluable resource for details of Hurston's life and works.

### Chapter 3: The Entanglement of Origins

1. Davis defines "races" as "categories of human beings based on average differences in physical traits that are transmitted by the genes . . ." and "an ethnic

group" as "a group with a sense of cultural identity . . . it may also be a racially distinctive group" (18). I will generally use the term "race" when discussing African Americans and "ethnicity" when referring to Irish people, but the matter is complicated by the fact that Irish people were once considered a race.

2. For the expression "taxi fallacy," see Gates, *Loose Canons,* 147.

3. As Davis points out, no other American ethnic group is defined by a one-drop rule, and no other countries, including South Africa under white rule, define blackness in this way (13).

4. African history has been similarly constructed as unitary in this century. See Oliver, *The African Experience,* 158 and chapter 12 in general.

5. Like many pre-1916 revolutionaries, Emmet was a Protestant, but the Catholic Pearse was comfortable invoking their names in a nationalistic religious context.

6. Cullen, *My Soul's High Song,* 105–6, lines 22, 26. All future references are to this edition.

7. See the work of Deane and Kiberd. Kiberd has moved away from this position, for example, in his lecture "Language, Writers, Texts," delivered on 13 July 1992 at the IASAIL conference on "Creativity and Its Contexts" at Trinity College, Dublin.

8. B. Anderson notes that this "otherwise persuasive thesis" does not apply to South and Central America. See *Imagined Communities,* 47–48.

9. Many participants in the Black Arts movement of the 1960s were critical of the Harlem Renaissance writers. See, for example, Cruse, *The Crisis of the Negro Intellectual,* 24–25. Huggins, on the other hand, describes them as the progressives of their time in *Harlem Renaissance,* 5–6.

10. J. Johnson, *The Autobiography of an Ex-Colored Man,* 195, and Larsen, *Passing,* 153. All future references are to these editions.

11. Fauset, *Plum Bun,* 13. All future references are to this edition.

12. Schuyler, *Black No More,* 23. All future references are to this edition. *Black No More* does not always jibe with other novels about passing because of its satirical nature.

13. Davis says this is extremely unlikely, but an important part of the mythology of passing (25).

14. Alice Dunbar-Nelson presents a somewhat different view in an essay written around 1929 entitled "Brass Ankles Speaks." It described the tribulations of a light-skinned woman who refuses to pass but who faces scorn nonetheless from her darker peers. Because an editor would not print it with a pseudonym, Dunbar-Nelson never published this essay. See Dunbar-Nelson, "Brass Ankles Speaks," 311–21.

15. Some black writers, for instance Jessie Fauset, reject racial essentialism in their writings about passing yet affirm it elsewhere in their work. See her essay "The Gift of Laughter." This inconsistency in addressing the meaning of blackness indicates how entrenched essentialism was in the early-twentieth-century zeitgeist.

## Chapter 4: Peril of Arrogance

1. The last sentence echoes Yeats's mentor, the Irish revolutionary John O'Leary, suggesting that the young poet had not yet completely worked through this issue.

2. This term should be read with inverted commas throughout, as it is largely a construction.

3. In *Gone Primitive*, 8–9, Torgovnick presents a similar definition for a term closely related to the folk—the primitive.

4. Mrs. Mason requested that the artists call her "Godmother."

5. Davis contrasts the Jamaican system, "where it is racial appearance that counts more than ancestry" to the American emphasis on ancestry. See *Who Is Black?* 125–26.

6. It is instructive to compare this passage to Yeats's comment about Paddy Flynn and note the recurrence of the words "instinctive" and "animal."

7. Du Bois used the image of Scylla and Charybdis to describe the difficult situation of the writers in "Harlem," 240.

8. Hughes later regretted the title of the book, which offended some Jewish people.

9. See also Rogers, "Rogers Calls," 4.

10. See, for example, Carby's critique of Hurston in *Reconstructing Womanhood* and Deane's depiction of Yeats in *Celtic Revivals*.

## Conclusion: Affirmative Actions

1. Patai offers another good definition of identity politics: "the assumption that a person's racial or ethnic identity and views are one and the same." See "The Struggle," B1. Although the intensity of identity politics is a feature of the second half of the twentieth century, it has been around for a long time: as Leverich points out, at the beginning of the nineteenth century, London critics frequently praised Anglo-Irish novelist Maria Edgeworth's representations of Irish people and scorned her depictions of London life simply because she was Irish—and despite the fact that she knew London much better than the Irish countryside.

2. Gates's example complicates the idea that subaltern peoples have easier access to their respective dominant cultures than vice versa: Milton's multiple subjectivity renders him at once the dominant culture and the subaltern—the blind Straight White Male.

3. Kimberly Benston is a notable exception to the self-consciousness phenomenon. See duCille, "Occult," 612–22, for an extended analysis.

4. The experience of African Americans vis-à-vis white writers is not unique: as Weisbuch relates in *Atlantic Double-cross*, European-American writers of the nineteenth and early twentieth centuries believed that they had to break free of an English literary tradition and establish an American one.

# Works Cited

Ahmad, Aijaz. *In Theory: Classes, Nations, Literatures.* London: Verso, 1992.

Allen, Theodore. *Racial Oppression and Social Control.* Vol. 1 of *The Invention of the White Race.* London: Verso, 1994.

Anderson, Benedict. *Imagined Communities: Reflections on the Origin and Spread of Nationalism.* Rev. ed. London: Verso, 1991.

Anderson, Jervis. *This Was Harlem.* New York: Farrar, Straus and Giroux, 1982.

Angelou, Maya. Interview with Paul Brown. National Public Radio broadcast, *Morning Edition,* 11 September 1992.

Archer, J. R. "Necessary Ambiguity: Nationalism and Myth in Ireland." *Éire-Ireland* 19.2 (1984): 23–37.

Baker, Houston A., Jr. "Caliban's Triple Play." *Critical Inquiry* 13.1 (1986): 182–96.

Bass, George Houston. "Another Bone of Contention: Reclaiming Our Gift of Laughter." In *Mule Bone: A Comedy of Negro Life,* by Zora Neale Hurston and Langston Hughes, edited by George Houston Bass and Henry Louis Gates, Jr., 1–4. New York: HarperCollins, 1991.

Beaumont, Gustave de. *Ireland: Social, Political, and Religious.* Vol. 1. London, 1839.

Beckett, J. C. *The Making of Modern Ireland 1603–1923.* 1966. New York: Knopf, 1983.

"Beginnings of a Negro Drama." *Literary Digest,* 9 May 1914, 1114.

Bennett, Lerone. *Before the Mayflower: A History of Black America.* New York: Penguin, 1993.

Berry, Faith. *Langston Hughes: Before and Beyond Harlem.* Westport, Conn.: L. Hill, 1983.

Bhabha, Homi K. "Of Mimicry and Men: The Ambivalence of Colonial Discourse." *October* 28 (1984): 125–33.

Blake, Susan L., and James A. Miller. "The Business of Writing: An Interview with David Bradley." *Callaloo* 7.2 (1984): 19–39.

Bornstein, George. "Afro-Celtic Connections: From Frederick Douglass to *The Commitments.*" In *Literary Influence and African-American Writers,* edited by Tracy Mishkin. New York: Garland, 1995.

Boucicault, Dion. Letter to the Editor. *London Times,* 20 November 1861, 5.

——. *Plays.* New York: Cambridge University Press, 1984.

Boyce, D. G. "The Marginal Britons: The Irish." In *Englishness: Politics and Culture 1880–1920,* edited by Robert Colls and Philip Dodd, 230–53. Dover, N.H.: Croom Helm, 1986.

Brawley, Benjamin. *The Negro Genius.* New York: Dodd, Mead, 1937.

——. *Paul Laurence Dunbar: Poet of His People.* Chapel Hill: University of North Carolina Press, 1936.

Broun, Heywood. "Negro Players Score Success in Interesting Bill of Short Plays." *New York Tribune,* 6 April 1917, 11.

Byrd, Rudolph. "Jean Toomer and the Afro-American Literary Tradition." *Callaloo* 24 (1985): 310–19.

Callahan, John. *In the African-American Grain: The Pursuit of Voice in Twentieth-Century Black Fiction.* Urbana: University of Illinois Press, 1988.

Carby, Hazel. *Reconstructing Womanhood: The Emergence of the Afro-American Woman Novelist.* New York: Oxford University Press, 1987.

Clifford, James. *The Predicament of Culture.* Cambridge, Mass.: Harvard University Press, 1988.

Cooper, Wayne F. *Claude McKay: Rebel Sojourner in the Harlem Renaissance.* Baton Rouge: Louisiana State University Press, 1987.

Corkery, Daniel. *Synge and Anglo-Irish Literature.* Cork: Cork University Press, 1931.

Cruse, Harold. *The Crisis of the Negro Intellectual.* New York: Morrow, 1967.

Cullen, Countee, ed. *Caroling Dusk.* 1927. New York: Harper, 1968.

——. "The Dark Tower." *Opportunity* 5 (1927): 180–81.

——. *My Soul's High Song: The Collected Writings of Countee Cullen, Voice of the Harlem Renaissance.* Edited by Gerald Early. New York: Doubleday, 1991.

——. *On These I Stand.* New York: Harper, 1947.

Curtis, Edmund. *A History of Ireland.* 6th ed. London: Methuen, 1950.

Curtis, L. Perry, Jr. *Apes and Angels: The Irishman in Victorian Caricature.* Washington, D.C.: Smithsonian Institution Press, 1971.

Dalsimer, Adele M. "Players in the Western World: The Abbey's Theatre's American Tours." *Éire-Ireland* 16 (1981): 75–93.

Darby, John. *Conflict in Northern Ireland: The Development of a Polarised Community.* New York: Barnes and Noble, 1976.

Davis, F. James. *Who Is Black? One Nation's Definition.* University Park: Pennsylvania State University Press, 1991.

Deane, Seamus. *Celtic Revivals: Essays in Modern Irish Literature 1880–1980.* London: Faber, 1985.

Delany, Martin R. *The Condition, Elevation, Emigration, and Destiny of the Colored People of the United States.* 1852. New York: Arno Press, 1968.

Dowden, Edward. *Letters of Edward Dowden and His Correspondents.* Edited by Elizabeth D. and Hilda Dowden. London: Dent, 1914.

Doyle, Roddy. *The Commitments.* 1987. New York: Vintage-Random, 1989; *The Commitments.* Directed by Alan Parker. 20th Century Fox, 1991.

Du Bois, W. E. B. "Criteria of Negro Art." *Crisis* 32 (1926): 290–97.

——. "England." *Crisis* 19 (1920): 107–8.

———. "England, Again." *Crisis* 19 (1920): 237–38.

———. "Harlem." *Crisis* 34 (1927): 240.

———. "Krigwa Players Little Negro Theatre." *Crisis* 32 (1926): 134.

———. "Returning Soldiers." *Crisis* 17 (1919): 13–14.

duCille, Ann. *The Coupling Convention: Sex, Text, and Tradition in Black Women's Fiction.* New York: Oxford University Press, 1993.

———. "The Occult of True Black Womanhood: Critical Demeanor and Black Feminist Studies." *Signs* 19 (1994): 588–629.

Dunbar, Paul Laurence. *The Complete Poems.* New York: Dodd, Mead, 1922.

———. *Sport of the Gods.* New York: Dodd, Mead, 1902.

Dunbar-Nelson, Alice. "Brass Ankles Speaks." In *The Works of Alice Dunbar-Nelson,* vol. 2, edited by Gloria T. Hull, 311–21. New York: Oxford University Press, 1988.

———. "Mine Eyes Have Seen." *Crisis* 15 (1918): 271–75.

Dunleavy, Janet Egleson, and Gareth W. Dunleavy. *Douglas Hyde: A Maker of Modern Ireland.* Berkeley: University of California Press, 1991.

Edmonds, Randolph. "Some Reflections on the Negro in American Drama." *Journal of Negro Life* 8 (1930): 303–5.

Ellison, Ralph. *Invisible Man.* New York: Random-Vintage, 1980.

Ellmann, Richard. *James Joyce.* Rev. ed. New York: Oxford University Press, 1982.

Fallis, Richard. *Irish Renaissance.* Syracuse: Syracuse University Press, 1977.

Fauset, Jessie. "The Gift of Laughter." In *The New Negro: An Interpretation,* edited by Alain Locke, 161–67. 1925. New York: Arno, 1968.

———. "The Negro in Art: How Shall He Be Portrayed? A Symposium." *Crisis* 32 (1926): 72.

———. "The New Books." *Crisis* 27 (1924): 174–77.

———. "Notes on the New Books." *Crisis* 25 (1923): 161–65.

———. *Plum Bun.* New York: Stokes, 1928.

Fawkes, Richard. *Dion Boucicault: A Biography.* London: Quartet, 1979.

Fennell, Desmond. "The Irish Language Movement: Its Achievements and Its Failure." *Twentieth Century Studies* (November 1970): 64–77.

Ferguson, Blanche. *Countee Cullen and the Negro Renaissance.* New York: Dodd, Mead, 1966.

Fishkin, Shelley Fisher. *Was Huck Black? Mark Twain and African-American Voices.* New York: Oxford University Press, 1993.

Foster, R. F. *Modern Ireland: 1600–1972.* New York: Penguin, 1988.

Freire, Paulo. *Pedagogy of the Oppressed.* Translated by Myra Bergman Ramos. New York: Herder, 1972.

Fuss, Diana. *Essentially Speaking.* New York: Routledge, 1989.

Gale, Zona. "The Colored Players and Their Plays." *Theatre Arts Magazine* 1 (1917): 139–40.

Gallagher, Brian. "About Us, For Us, Near Us: The Irish and Harlem Renaissances." *Éire-Ireland* 16.4 (1981): 14–26.

Gates, Henry Louis, Jr. *Colored People: A Memoir.* New York: Knopf, 1994.

———. *Figures in Black: Words, Signs, and the "Racial" Self.* New York: Oxford University Press, 1987.

———. *Loose Canons: Notes on the Culture Wars.* New York: Oxford University Press, 1992.

————. "A Tragedy of Negro Life." In *Mule Bone: A Comedy of Negro Life,* by Zora Neale Hurston and Langston Hughes; edited by George Houston Bass and Henry Louis Gates, Jr., 5–24. New York: HarperCollins, 1991.

Gellner, Ernest. *Nations and Nationalism.* Oxford: Blackwell, 1983.

Genovese, Eugene D. *Roll, Jordan, Roll: The World the Slaves Made.* New York: Pantheon-Random, 1974.

Gibbons, Luke. "Race Against Time: Racial Discourse and Irish History." *Oxford Literary Review* 13 (1991): 95–117.

Gilley, Sheridan. "English Attitudes to the Irish in England: 1780–1900." In *Immigrants and Minorities in British Society,* edited by Colin Holmes, 81–110. London: Allen, 1978.

Greene, David H. "Robert Atkinson and Irish Studies." *Hermathena* 102 (1966): 6–15.

Greene, David H., and Edward M. Stephens. *J. M. Synge 1871–1909.* Rev. ed. New York: New York University Press, 1989.

Gregory, Augusta. *Cuchulain of Muirthemne.* 1902. London: Murray, 1915.

————. *Gods and Fighting Men.* 1904. London: Murray, 1905.

————. *Our Irish Theatre.* New York: Putnam, 1913.

————. *Seventy Years: Being the Autobiography of Lady Gregory.* Gerrards Cross, Buckinghamshire: Smythe, 1974.

Griffith, Arthur. Preface. In *Jail Journal,* by John Mitchel. Dublin: Gill, 1913.

Hale, Anthony. Personal communication, May 1996.

Hatch, James V., ed. *Black Theater, U.S.A.: Forty-five Plays by Black Americans 1847–1974.* New York: Macmillan, 1974.

Hayden, Robert. *Collected Prose.* Ann Arbor: University of Michigan Press, 1984.

Heaney, Seamus. "The Interesting Case of John Alphonsus Mulrennan." *Planet* 41 (1978): 34–40.

Hemenway, Robert. *Zora Neale Hurston: A Literary Biography.* Urbana: University of Illinois Press, 1977.

Hill, Robert A., ed. *The Marcus Garvey and Universal Negro Improvement Association Papers.* Vol. 2. Berkeley: University of California Press, 1983.

Hirsch, Edward. "The Imaginary Irish Peasant." *PMLA* 106 (1991): 1116–33.

Holloway, Joseph. *Joseph Holloway's Abbey Theatre.* Edited by Robert Hogan and Michael J. O'Neill. Carbondale: Southern Illinois University Press, 1967.

"The Housing of the Very Poor." *British Medical Journal,* 9 May 1903, 1108.

Howells, William Dean. Introduction to *Lyrics of Lowly Life.* In *The Complete Poems,* by Paul Laurence Dunbar, vii-x. New York: Dodd, Mead, 1922.

————. "Life and Letters." *Harper's Weekly,* 27 June 1896, 630.

Hudson, Gossie H. "Paul Laurence Dunbar: Dialect et la Negritude." *Phylon* 34 (1973): 236–47.

Huggins, Nathan Irvin. *Harlem Renaissance.* New York: Oxford University Press, 1971.

————, ed. *Voices from the Harlem Renaissance.* New York: Oxford University Press, 1976.

Hughes, Langston. *The Big Sea.* New York: Knopf, 1940.

————. *The Collected Poems of Langston Hughes.* Edited by Arnold Rampersad. New York: Knopf, 1995.

————. *Fight for Freedom: The Story of the NAACP.* New York: Norton, 1962.

————. "The Negro Artist and the Racial Mountain." *Nation* 23 (June 1926): 692–94.

————. "These Bad New Negroes: A Critique on Critics." *Pittsburgh Courier,* 9 April 1927, natl. ed., sec. 2, p. 1; 16 April 1927, sec. 1, p. 8.

Hunt, Hugh. *The Abbey: Ireland's National Theatre.* Dublin: Gill, 1979.

Hurston, Zora Neale. *Dust Tracks on a Road.* 1942. Urbana: University of Illinois Press, 1984.

————. "How It Feels to Be Colored Me." In her *I Love Myself When I Am Laughing,* edited by Alice Walker, 152–55. New York: Feminist, 1979.

————. *Moses, Man of the Mountain.* 1939. Urbana: University of Illinois Press, 1984.

————. *Mules and Men.* 1935. New York: Harper, 1990.

————. *Their Eyes Were Watching God.* 1937. Urbana: University of Illinois Press, 1978.

Hurston, Zora Neale, and Langston Hughes. *Mule Bone: A Comedy of Negro Life.* Edited by George Houston Bass and Henry Louis Gates, Jr. New York: HarperCollins, 1991.

Hutchinson, George. *The Harlem Renaissance in Black and White.* Cambridge, Mass.: Belknap-Harvard University Press, 1995.

Hyde, Douglas. *Language, Lore, and Lyrics: Essays and Lectures.* Edited by Breandán Ó Conaire. Dublin: Irish Academic Press, 1986.

————. *Love Songs of Connacht.* 1893. Shannon: Irish University Press, 1969.

Hyman, Louis. *The Jews of Ireland from Earliest Times to the Year 1910.* Shannon: Irish University Press, 1972.

Innes, C. L. *The Devil's Own Mirror: The Irishman and the African in Modern Literature.* Washington, D.C.: Three Continents Press, 1990.

Jacobs, Harriet. *Incidents in the Life of a Slave Girl.* Edited by Jean Fagan Yellin. Cambridge, Mass.: Harvard University Press, 1987.

Johnson, Barbara. *A World of Difference.* Baltimore: Johns Hopkins University Press, 1987.

Johnson, Charles. "The New Frontage on American Life." In *The New Negro: An Interpretation,* edited by Alain Locke, 278–98. 1925. New York: Arno, 1968.

Johnson, James Weldon. *Along This Way.* New York: Viking, 1933.

————. *The Autobiography of an Ex-Colored Man.* 1912. New York: Vintage-Random, 1989.

————. *God's Trombones: Seven Negro Sermons in Verse.* 1927. New York: Viking-Penguin, 1990.

————. "The Negro and the Drama." *New York Age,* 19 April 1917, n. p.

————. "Prejudice Minus Discrimination." *New York Age,* 28 January 1915, n. p.

————. "Prejudice in the National Guard." *New York Age,* 22 June 1916, n. p.

————. "Why the Difference?" *New York Age,* 3 February 1916, n. p.

————, ed. *The Book of American Negro Poetry.* New York: Harcourt, 1922.

Jones, Gayl. *Liberating Voices: Oral Tradition in African American Literature.* Cambridge, Mass.: Harvard University Press, 1991.

Joyce, James. "The Dead." In his *Dubliners,* 175–224. New York: Modern Library, 1967.

————. *Ulysses.* New York: Vintage-Random, 1961.

Kaufman, Jonathan. *Broken Alliance: The Turbulent Times Between Blacks and Jews in America.* New York: Scribner, 1988.

Kearney, Richard. "Migrant Minds." Interview with Bono. In *Across the Frontiers: Ireland in the 1990s,* 188–91. Dublin: Wolfhound, 1988.

Kenner, Hugh. *A Colder Eye: The Modern Irish Writers.* New York: Knopf, 1983.

———. Foreword to *"Dear, Dirty Dublin": A City in Distress, 1899–1916,* by Joseph V. O'Brien, vii–x. Berkeley: University of California Press, 1982.

Kerman, Cynthia Earl, and Richard Eldridge. *The Lives of Jean Toomer: A Hunger for Wholeness.* Baton Rouge: Louisiana State University Press, 1987.

Kiberd, Declan. "Language, Writers, Texts." "Creativity and Its Contexts." IASAIL conference, Trinity College, Dublin, 13 July 1992.

———. *Synge and the Irish Language.* London: Macmillan, 1979.

Kingsley, Charles. *His Letters and Memories of His Life.* Edited by Fanny Kingsley. Abr. ed. New York: Scribner, 1877.

Kinsella, Thomas. *The Tain.* 1969. London: Oxford University Press, 1970.

Kirchwey, Freda. Review of *Banjo,* by Claude McKay. *Nation,* 22 May 1929, 614ff.

Kohfeldt, Mary Lou. *Lady Gregory: The Woman Behind the Irish Renaissance.* New York: Atheneum, 1985.

"Langston Hughes—the Sewer Dweller." Review of *Fine Clothes to the Jew,* by Langston Hughes. *Amsterdam News* [New York], 9 February 1927, 22.

Larsen, Nella. *Quicksand* and *Passing.* 1928. New Brunswick, N.J.: Rutgers University Press, 1986.

Lawson, Victor. *Dunbar Critically Examined.* Washington, D.C.: Associated Publishers, 1941.

Leerssen, Joep. "Tain After Tain: The Mythical Past and the Anglo-Irish." In *History and Violence in Anglo-Irish Literature,* edited by Joris Duytschaever and Geert Lernout, 29–46. Amsterdam: Rodopi, 1988.

Lester, Julius. "The Outsiders: Blacks and Jews and the Soul of America." *Transition* 5.4 (1995): 66–88.

Leverich, Jean. "Maria Edgeworth's *Castle Rackrent* and the Function of Regionalism." Paper given at the Midwest Meeting of the American Conference on Irish Studies, Carbondale, Ill., October 1992.

Lewis, David L. *When Harlem Was in Vogue.* 1981. New York: Oxford University Press, 1989.

Locke, Alain. "Jingo, Counter-Jingo and Us." Review of *Their Eyes Were Watching God,* by Zora Neale Hurston. *Opportunity* 16.1 (1938): 7ff.

———. "Negro Youth Speaks." In *The New Negro: An Interpretation,* edited by Locke, 47–53. 1925. New York: Arno, 1968.

———. "The New Negro." Introduction to *The New Negro: An Interpretation,* edited by Locke, 3–16. 1925. New York: Arno, 1968.

Locke, Alain, and Montgomery Gregory, eds. *Plays of Negro Life.* New York: Harper, 1927.

Lovejoy, Arthur O., and George Boas. *A Documentary History of Primitivism and Related Ideas.* Vol. 1. Baltimore: Johns Hopkins University Press, 1935.

Lyons, F. S. L. *Culture and Anarchy in Ireland.* Oxford: Clarendon, 1979.

MacDonagh, Thomas. *Literature in Ireland.* London: Fisher, 1916.

MacKethan, Lucinda H. "Plantation Fiction, 1865–1900." In *The History of Southern Literature,* edited by Louis D. Rubin, Jr., 209–18. Baton Rouge: Louisiana State University Press, 1985.

MacLochlainn, Alf. "Gael and Peasant: A Case of Mistaken Identity?" In *Views of the Irish Peasantry 1800–1916,* edited by Daniel J. Casey and Robert E. Rhodes, 17–36. Hamden, Conn.: Archon, 1977.

Marcus, Philip. *Yeats and the Beginning of the Irish Renaissance.* Ithaca: Cornell University Press, 1970.

Martin, F. X. "Diarmait Mac Murchada and the Coming of the Anglo-Normans." In *A New History of Ireland: Medieval Ireland 1169–1534,* vol. 2, edited by Art Cosgrove, 43–66. Oxford: Clarendon Press, 1993.

McDowell, Deborah. "Lines of Descent/Dissenting Lines." Foreword to *Moses Man of the Mountain,* by Zora Neale Hurston, vii–xxii. New York: HarperPerennial, 1991.

McGregor, Gaile. *The Noble Savage in the New World Garden: Notes Towards a Syntactics of Place.* Bowling Green, Ohio: Bowling Green University Press, 1988.

McKay, Claude. "Boyhood in Jamaica." *Phylon* 13 (1953): 134–45.

———. "Claude M'Kay Tells of Jews." *Amsterdam News* [New York], 24 December 1938, 17.

———. *Dialect Poetry.* Freeport, N.Y.: Books for Libraries, 1972.

———. *Home to Harlem.* 1928. New York: Pocket Books, 1965.

———. "How Black Sees Green and Red." In *The Passion of Claude McKay,* edited by Wayne Cooper, 57–62. New York: Schocken, 1973.

———. *A Long Way from Home.* New York: Furman, 1937.

———. *Selected Poems of Claude McKay.* New York: Bookman, 1953.

McMillan, Terry. Introduction to *Breaking Ice: An Anthology of Contemporary African-American Fiction.* New York: Penguin, 1990.

Meier, August. *Negro Thought in America, 1880–1915: Racial Ideologies in the Age of Booker T. Washington.* Ann Arbor: University of Michigan Press, 1963.

Mitchel, John. *Jail Journal.* Dublin: Gill, 1913.

Morrison, Toni. *Playing in the Dark: Whiteness and the Literary Imagination.* Cambridge, Mass.: Harvard University Press, 1992.

Muldoon, Paul. *Selected Poems.* London: Faber, 1986.

Murphy, Daniel. Foreword to *Cuchulain of Muirthemne,* by Augusta Gregory. Gerrards Cross, Buckinghamshire: Smythe, 1970.

Murphy, Maureen. "Lady Gregory and the Gaelic League." In *Lady Gregory, Fifty Years After,* edited by Ann Saddlemyer and Colin Smythe, 143–62. Gerrards Cross, Buckinghamshire: Smythe, 1987.

Nadel, Ira B. *Joyce and the Jews: Culture and Texts.* Iowa City: University of Iowa Press, 1989.

Nairn, Tom. *The Break-up of Britain: Crisis and Neo-Nationalism.* Rev. ed. London: Verso, 1981.

Nast, Thomas. "The Ignorant Vote: Honors Are Easy." Cover illustration. *Harper's Weekly,* 9 December 1876.

"The New Negro Theatre." *Crisis* 14 (1917): 80–81.

Nielsen, Aldon L. *Writing Between the Lines: Race and Intertextuality.* Athens: University of Georgia Press, 1994.

O'Brien, Conor Cruise. *States of Ireland.* New York: Random-Pantheon, 1972.

O'Brien, Joseph V. *"Dear, Dirty Dublin": A City in Distress, 1899–1916.* Berkeley: University of California Press, 1982.

O'Connor, Ulick. *All The Olympians: A Biographical Portrait of the Irish Literary Renaissance.* New York: Atheneum, 1984.

"'The Octoroon.' A Disgrace to the North, a Libel on the South." Review of *The Octoroon,* by Dion Boucicault. *Spirit of the Times,* 17 December 1859, 1.

O'Ferrall, Fergus. "Liberty and Catholic Politics 1790–1990." In *Daniel O'Connell: Political Pioneer,* edited by Maurice O'Connell, 35–56. Dublin: Institute of Public Administration, 1991.

O'Grady, Standish James. *Selected Essays and Passages.* Dublin: Talbot, 1918.

Okeke-Ezigbo, Emeka. "Paul Laurence Dunbar: Straightening the Record." *College Language Association Journal* 24 (1981): 481–96.

Oliver, Roland. *The African Experience.* New York: HarperCollins, 1991.

Osofsky, Gilbert. *Harlem: The Making of a Ghetto.* New York: Harper, 1966.

O'Sullivan, Maurice J., Jr., and Jack C. Lane. "Zora Neale Hurston at Rollins College." In *Zora in Florida,* edited by Steve Glassman and Kathryn Lee Seidel, 130–45. Orlando: University of Central Florida Press, 1991.

Patai, Daphne. "The Struggle for Feminist Purity Threatens the Goals of Feminism." *Chronicle of Higher Education,* 5 February 1992, B1–2.

Patterson, Nerys, and Orlando Patterson. "St. Patrick Was A Slave." *New York Times,* 15 March 1993, A19.

Pearse, Patrick. *Political Writings and Speeches,* vol. 3 of *The Collected Works of Pádraig H. Pearse.* Edited by Desmond Ryan and Patrick Brown. Dublin: Phoenix, 1924.

Randolph, A. Phillip. "A New Crowd—A New Negro." In *Voices from the Harlem Renaissance,* edited by Nathan Huggins, 18–20. New York: Oxford University Press, 1976.

Rich, Frank. "Synge's 'Playboy,' Moved to Trinidad." *New York Times,* 10 May 1993, B1ff.

Richardson, Willis. "The Hope of a Negro Drama." *Crisis* 19 (1919): 338–39.

———, ed. *Plays and Pageants from the Life of the Negro.* Washington, D.C.: Associated Publishers, 1930.

Richardson, Willis, and May Miller, eds. *Negro History in Thirteen Plays.* Washington, D.C.: Associated Publishers, 1935.

Rogers, J. A. "Rogers Calls Langston Hughes' Book of Poems 'Trash.'" Review of *Fine Clothes to the Jew,* by Langston Hughes. *Pittsburgh Courier,* 12 February 1927, natl. ed., sec. 1, p. 4.

Rolston, Bill. "Politics, Painting, and Popular Culture: The Political Wall Murals of Northern Ireland." *Media, Culture, and Society* 9 (1987): 5–28.

Saddlemyer, Ann. *In Defence of Lady Gregory, Playwright.* Dublin: Dolmen, 1966.

Said, Edward. *Orientalism.* 1978. New York: Vintage-Random, 1979.

Sanders, Leslie Catherine. *The Development of Black Theater in America: From Shadows to Selves.* Baton Rouge: Louisiana State University Press, 1988.

Schomberg, Arthur. "The Negro Digs Up His Past." In *Voices from the Harlem Renaissance,* edited by Nathan Huggins, 217–21. New York: Oxford University Press, 1976.

Schuyler, George. *Black No More.* New York: Macauley, 1931.

———. "The Negro-Art Hokum." *Nation,* 16 June 1926, 662–63.

Simon, Myron. "Dunbar and Dialect Poetry." In *A Singer in the Dawn: Reinterpretations of Paul Laurence Dunbar,* edited by Jay Martin, 114–34. New York: Dodd, Mead, 1975.

Sollors, Werner. Introduction to *The Invention of Ethnicity,* edited by Werner Sollors, ix–x. New York: Oxford University Press, 1989.

Sowell, Thomas. *Ethnic America.* New York: Basic, 1981.

Stanford, W. B., and R. B. McDowell. *Mahaffy: A Biography of an Anglo-Irishman.* London: Routledge, 1971.

Stein, Judith. "Defining the Race 1890–1930." In *The Invention of Ethnicity*, edited by Werner Sollors, 77–104. New York: Oxford University Press, 1989.

Sundquist, Eric. *To Wake the Nations: Race in the Making of American Literature.* Cambridge, Mass.: Belknap-Harvard University Press, 1993.

Sylvander, Carolyn Wedin. *Jessie Redmon Fauset, Black American Writer.* Troy, N.Y.: Whitston, 1981.

Synge, John. *The Collected Letters of John Millington Synge.* Vol. 1. Edited by Ann Saddlemyer. Oxford: Clarendon Press, 1983.

———. *The Complete Plays of John M. Synge.* New York: Vintage-Random, 1960.

———. *The Works of John M. Synge.* Vol. 3, *The Aran Islands.* Dublin: Maunsel, 1910.

Spenser, Edmund. *The Works of Edmund Spenser*, edited by Rudolf Gottfried. Vol. 9. Baltimore: Johns Hopkins University Press, 1949.

Thompson, Vincent Bakpetu. *The Making of the African Diaspora in the Americas, 1441–1900.* New York: Longman, 1987.

Thornton, Weldon. *Allusions in Ulysses: An Annotated List.* Chapel Hill: University of North Carolina Press, 1968.

Thuente, Mary Helen. *The Harp Re-strung: The United Irishmen and the Rise of Irish Literary Nationalism.* Syracuse: Syracuse University Press, 1994.

Thurman, Wallace. *Infants of the Spring.* 1932. New York: AMS, 1975.

Toomer, Jean. *Cane.* New York: Liveright, 1951.

Torgovnick, Marianna. *Gone Primitive: Modern Intellects, Savage Lives.* Chicago: Chicago University Press, 1990.

Torrence, Ridgely. *Granny Maumee, The Rider of Dreams, Simon the Cyrenian: Plays for a Negro Theatre.* New York: Macmillan, 1917.

Turner, Darwin T. Introduction to *Cane*, by Jean Toomer. New York: Liveright, 1973, ix–xxv.

———. "Paul Laurence Dunbar: The Poet and the Myths." In *A Singer in the Dawn: Reinterpretations of Paul Laurence Dunbar*, edited by Jay Martin, 59–74. New York: Dodd, Mead, 1975.

Van Vechten, Carl. *Nigger Heaven.* New York: Knopf, 1926.

Walker, Alice. *In Search of Our Mothers' Gardens.* New York: Harcourt, 1983.

Walton, Lester A. "Negro Actors Make Debut in Drama at Garden Theatre; Given Most Cordial Welcome." *New York Age,* 12 April 1917, n. p.

———. "Theatrical Comment." *New York Age,* 25 November 1909, n. p.

———. "Using the Real Thing." *New York Age,* 5 October 1911, n. p.

Warren, Kenneth. *Black and White Strangers: Race and American Literary Realism.* Chicago: University of Chicago Press, 1993.

Waters, Mary. *Ethnic Options: Choosing Identities in America.* Berkeley: University of California Press, 1990.

Weinberg, Meyer, ed. *The World of W. E. B. Du Bois: A Quotation Sourcebook.* Westport, Conn.: Greenwood Press, 1992.

Weisbuch, Robert. *Atlantic Double-cross: American Literature and British Influence in the Age of Emerson.* Chicago: University of Chicago Press, 1986.

Welch, Robert. "A Language for Healing." In *Lady Gregory, Fifty Years After*, edited by Ann Saddlemyer and Colin Smythe, 258–73. Gerrards Cross, Buckinghamshire: Smythe, 1987.

Winkler, Karen J. "A Scholar's Provocative Query: Was Huckleberry Finn Black?" *Chronicle of Higher Education,* 8 July 1992, A7–8.

Wintz, Cary D. *Black Culture and the Harlem Renaissance.* Houston: Rice University Press, 1988.

Woolf, Virginia. "Mr. Bennett and Mrs. Brown." In her *Collected Essays,* vol. 1. New York: Harcourt, Brace, 1967, 319–37.

Wright, Donald R. *African Americans in the Colonial Era: From African Origins Through the American Revolution.* Arlington Heights, Ill: Davidson, 1990.

Wright, Richard. "Between Laughter and Tears." Review of *Their Eyes Were Watching God,* by Zora Neale Hurston. *New Masses* 25 (1937): 22ff.

Yeats, W. B. *Autobiographies.* London: Macmillan, 1955.

———. *The Celtic Twilight.* London, 1893.

———. *Essays and Introductions.* London: Macmillan, 1961.

———. *Explorations.* London: Macmillan, 1962.

———. *Letters to the New Island.* Vol. 7 of *The Collected Works of W. B. Yeats.* Edited George Bornstein and Hugh Witemeyer. New York: Macmillan, 1989.

———. *The Poems.* Rev. ed. Vol. 1 of *The Collected Works of W. B. Yeats.* Edited by Richard J. Finneran. New York: Macmillan, 1989.

# Index

Abbey Theatre: and African Americans 16, 17, 18; and Carolina Playmakers 109n.1; and controversy 1, 16, 17, 21, 89, 97; and Little Theatre movement 14, 109n.1; and stereotypes 12, 14, 89; and Synge 17; tours United States 1, 2, 16, 21, 23. *See also* Irish theater

Africa: black attitudes toward 44, 74; history 112n.4; influence of geography on slavery 26

Anglo-Irish: commitment of, questioned 75–76; decline of 30–31, 76; definition of 29–30; development of identity 30; rejected by Catholic nationalists 67, 86; revivers of Irish culture 33, 37, 38–39, 76; similarity to Southern slaveowners 31; Yeats's construction of tradition 70, 76. *See also* Irish Catholics

Aran Islands: folklore translated by Synge 55; material success and folk culture 91

Ascendancy. *See also* Anglo-Irish

Catholic emancipation: and Anglo-Irish 30; and slavery 10; impact of 28, 30, 34. *See also* Penal Laws

Catholics, Irish: Anglo-Irish fear of 29; dispossession by Penal Laws 27–28; in Gaelic League 35; in Irish Revolutionary Brotherhood 42; Jews not considered Irish by 6; middle class abandonment of poor 40; nationalist activity 34, 71; pressure on writers 99; struggle for civil rights 23, 102. *See also* Anglo-Irish; Nationalism; Penal Laws

Civil rights: importance of literature to 89;

Irish Catholic 23, 102; Jews aid black struggle for 3; of nineteenth-century free blacks 28; and stereotypes 32. See also Emancipation; Prejudice, Propaganda; Stereotypes

Communism: and African Americans 45; impact on writers 64; and NAACP 44; and New Negroes 37; and UNIA 44. *See also* Labor movement; Socialism

Colonialism: common ground for McKay and Irish 20, 22; common ground for South Africans and Northern Irish Catholics 103; and racial meaning of word "plantation" 110n.1.

Cullen, Countee: ambivalence toward Africa 74; meets Irish poets 18; and interracial influence 106; and racial identity 77–78

Dialects, African-American: and Dunbar 57–60; and Hurston 62–64; and Johnson 16–17; and McKay 60–62; and shame 48, 57; and slaves 56–57; and Torrence 15

Dialects, Irish: and Abbey Theatre 12; and Lady Gregory 53–54; and Hyde 51–52; and Irish Renaissance writers 47, 65; and Synge 17, 54–56

Douglass, Frederick: and Jews 4; and Irish 10, 11.

Dublin: and Anglo-Norman settlement 25; living conditions 39–40, 41; and migration 37; role compared to Harlem 16, 111n.11

Du Bois, W. E. B.: black-Irish comparisons by 19; and black theater 14, 16; on

Pseudo-science: and black-Irish comparisons 12; and essentialism 67; and
stereotypes 31. *See also* Nast

Richardson, Willis: and audience 7; black-
Irish comparison 16; and essentialism
73; and propaganda 16, 88

Sinn Fein: and Joyce 8; and African
Americans 19, 20, 103. *See also*
Nationalism
Slaves: and Anglo-Irish 31; and Dunbar
58–60; and free blacks 31; and Irish 9–
12, 19, 33, 103, 109n.1; and Jews 3;
and language 26, 47, 56–57, 110n.4;
and literature 97–98; living conditions
28; and stereotypes 32. *See also*
Emancipation
Socialism: and African Americans 19–20,
45; impact on writers 64; Irish 43; and
Jews 3; and New Negroes 37; and UNIA
44. *See also* Labor movement; Communism
South Africa: definition of blackness
112n.3; minority rule compared to Penal
Laws 110n.5; wall murals 103
Spiritualism 71, 92
Spirituals: and Jews 3; and Johnson 83, 94;
and black self-image 97, 98
Standard English: and African-Americans
writers 64–65; and Dunbar 57, 60; and
Johnson 17; and McKay 60–62; and
slaves 56–57; and Synge 55
Stereotypes: of African Americans 22,
110n.4; and dialect literature 56; and
dominant culture 31–32; and Hurston
62, 63; in interracial comparisons 9, 23,
31–32; of Jews 4, 9; in popular
entertainment 62, 63, 110n.4. *See also*
Civil Rights; Essentialism; Prejudice
Synge, John: and Anglo-Irish nationalism
75; and controversy 1, 17–18, 56, 70,
99, 111n.6; and dialect literature 54–56;
and African Americans 15, 16, 17–18,
103; and Irish literature 38, 110n.10;
and *Playboy* 1; and primitivism 70–71,
91–92, 943

Theater, African-American: and dialect 15;
and Du Bois 14, 16; and Irish theater
14, 15, 16; and Jewish theater 7; and
propaganda 16, 88; and Richardson 7,
16, 73, 88; and Torrence 14–16, 20
Theater, Irish: and African Americans 15,
16; and Hyde 50; and Torrence 14, 20.
*See also* Abbey Theatre
Toomer, Jean: and primitivism 100; and
racial identity 78–80

Urban League: and Jews 3; journal reviews
Hughes favorably; moves to Harlem 38.
*See also* NAACP

Van Vechten, Carl: black-Irish comparison
15; characters' attitudes towards Africa
74; depiction of Harlem 40
Violence, racial: and black resistance 36;
Ku Klux Klan 29, 45, 88, 95; migration
33–34; and propaganda 88; after
Reconstruction 29

Washington, D.C.: and Harlem 38; and
black self-defense 36; as original black
capital 33
West Indians: and Irish literature 103;
immigration to New York 41; McKay
60–62, 95–96; and racial identity
113n.5
World War I: black attitudes toward 9, 44;
and black self-image 36; and blood
sacrifice rhetoric 43; and Irish politics
42; and racial violence 33, 36

Yeats, W. B.: and Abbey Theatre 12, 14;
and African Americans 20–21, 23; and
Anglo-Irish 76; and dominant culture
stereotypes 12, 14; and folklore 37–38,
51–52, 53; and Hyde 51–52; and Irish
identity 69–70, 71, 76, 81, 82; and Irish
language 50; and politics 34–35, 40, 89,
113n.1; and primitivism 92–93, 113n.6;
and propaganda 86–87; and spiritualism
71, 92
Young Ireland: and slavery 10; and Anglo-
Irish 31; and nationalism 35.

Tracy Mishkin is assistant professor of English at Georgia College and State University, Milledgeville. She is the editor of a volume of essays, *Literary Influence and African-American Writers* (1996).